T0367015

The Cybersecurity Manager's Guide

The Art of Building Your Security Program

Todd Barnum

Beijing · Boston · Farnham · Sebastopol · Tokyo

The Cybersecurity Manager's Guide

by Todd Barnum

Published by O'Reilly Media, Inc., 1005 Gravenstein Highway North, Sebastopol, CA 95472.

O'Reilly books may be purchased for educational, business, or sales promotional use. Online editions are also available for most titles (*http://oreilly.com*). For more information, contact our corporate/institutional sales department: 800-998-9938 or *corporate@oreilly.com*.

Acquisitions Editor: Mary Preap	**Indexer:** WordCo Indexing Services, Inc.
Development Editor: Amelia Blevins	**Interior Designer:** Monica Kamsvaag
Production Editor: Caitlin Ghegan	**Cover Designer:** Randy Comer
Copyeditor: Sharon Wilkey	**Illustrator:** Kate Dullea
Proofreader: Sonia Saruba	

March 2021:   First Edition

Revision History for the First Edition

2021-03-25:   First Release

See *http://oreilly.com/catalog/errata.csp?isbn=9781492076216* for release details.

978-1-492-07621-6

[LSI]

Contents

Why I Wrote this Book

In January 2000, I started my first corporate information security (InfoSec) position after serving in the military. I had no appreciation for the cultural differences between the military and corporate life—in particular, the views and attitudes toward InfoSec. My assumption was that cybersecurity (I use this term interchangeably with *information security*) anywhere was still cybersecurity, and naturally valued by all. Boy, was I in for a shock. I had more sleepless nights in my first year of corporate life than I had sailing the Persian Gulf during a time of armed conflict.

While writing this book, I've made the assumption that you are very well versed in the eight domains of InfoSec. Many will ask why I mention the eight domains when we have so many industry frameworks that enumerate the various facets of our profession. The difference between the industry frameworks and the eight domains is that the former is a set of security controls by topic area, whereas the eight domains provide descriptions of those topics. The two are fundamentally different.

What you're holding in your hands is a culmination of my learning over the past 25 years. I've learned that InfoSec is vastly different from one company to the next. And, although there is a *science* aspect to our field, as outlined in the eight domains, the *art* of our profession is far less understood by us in the industry. Yet this nuanced art side, seldom (if ever) discussed within our profession, is just as important, if not more important, than the science side. I like to call this art side the *last domain* of InfoSec.

This book presents this art side of our field through a simple seven-step process focused on the essential elements in building an InfoSec program. These seven steps contain the basic formula for success, whether you're a new or well-established security leader. They are applicable to programs up and down the maturity scale, and are best used if you're building an InfoSec program from scratch or revisiting an already existing program you inherited from your predecessor.

A lot of important security topics are not mentioned in this book. This book, however, is not intended to be a technical manual or comprehensive guide for security leaders, but to provide a basic road map of key activities to guide you—whether you're building a new InfoSec program or revisiting an already established program. I hope you enjoy the book.

Conventions Used in This Book

The following typographical conventions are used in this book:

Italic

> Indicates new terms, URLs, email addresses, filenames, and file extensions.

`Constant width`

> Used for program listings, as well as within paragraphs to refer to program elements such as variable or function names, databases, data types, environment variables, statements, and keywords.

O'Reilly Online Learning

 For more than 40 years, *O'Reilly Media* has provided technology and business training, knowledge, and insight to help companies succeed.

Our unique network of experts and innovators share their knowledge and expertise through books, articles, and our online learning platform. O'Reilly's online learning platform gives you on-demand access to live training courses, in-depth learning paths, interactive coding environments, and a vast collection of text and video from O'Reilly and 200+ other publishers. For more information, visit *http://oreilly.com*.

How to Contact Us

Please address comments and questions concerning this book to the publisher:

> O'Reilly Media, Inc.
>
> 1005 Gravenstein Highway North
>
> Sebastopol, CA 95472

800-998-9938 (in the United States or Canada)

707-829-0515 (international or local)

707-829-0104 (fax)

We have a web page for this book, where we list errata, examples, and any additional information. You can access this page at *https://oreil.ly/Cybersecurity_Managers_Guide*.

Email *bookquestions@oreilly.com* to comment or ask technical questions about this book.

For news and information about our books and courses, visit http://oreilly.com.

Find us on Facebook: *http://facebook.com/oreilly*

Follow us on Twitter: *http://twitter.com/oreillymedia*

Watch us on YouTube: *http://www.youtube.com/oreillymedia*

Acknowledgments

I couldn't have written this book without the help of Ron Dilley, whom I had the pleasure of working with from 2000 to 2011. Ron was my thought partner throughout the writing of this book and contributed much to the book's contents. To Tim Mather, who introduced me to the O'Reilly team. To Amelia Blevins, my O'Reilly editor, who suffered through the many iterations and rewrites, yet always remained encouraging. Thanks also to my technical reviewers for their feedback and guidance—Dean Bushmiller, Geoffrey Hill, Michelle Ribeiro, and Glenn Wilson. To the entire O'Reilly team (especially Sharon Wilkey) who pulled this all together. My heartfelt thanks to you all.

The Odds Are Against You

Before I lay out my road map for building or revisiting an information security program, let me first provide some context of the environment in which most of us work. I say *most* because some of us have the privilege of working in companies with great executive sponsorship. These companies greatly value InfoSec for what it provides to the company in protecting its intellectual property. They understand the value the function provides, and view InfoSec as integral to the fabric of the organization. For the rest of us, we stand on soft soil. If I'm being honest about our situation, we're on our own when it comes to building out the InfoSec program. Neither the culture nor any executive sponsor will provide much support. The work of putting the program in place rests solely on the security leader. I liken it to pushing a boulder up a hill. The forces are against you.

The context I'm about to share has been my experience working as a security leader in various organizations. I've always been one to learn from others, keeping my ear tuned to the latest trends, while challenging the InfoSec industry's accepted standard practices. Over the years, I've realized that most of us operate in a work environment framed by a few fundamental facts. These facts are true for the vast majority of us, except for those chosen few who work with strong executive sponsors, almost unlimited resources, and a company culture favorable to InfoSec. Here are those facts:

1. Nobody in the company, outside of your team, usually cares much about InfoSec.
2. Nobody in the company really understands your job.
3. Our industry is guided by fear and scare tactics.

My conclusions about our operating environment stem from considering the many disconnects we confront every day in our jobs. For example, the number one security control in every framework is *asset enumeration*. And everyone agrees this is the most important security control and where all security starts. Yet, how many of us work at organizations that take this seriously? How many of you have gotten your arms around asset enumeration? Right? This is good data: the first and most important security control is almost completely ignored where you work. Has it ever been a sustained priority by your systems leadership? This doesn't seem odd to you? But the question is, what does it tell you?

Or consider the *tone from the top*. Everyone agrees this is super important for a successful InfoSec program. But when was the last time anyone was disciplined, let alone fired, for InfoSec policy violations? Unlike codes of conduct or human resources (HR) policies, which are strictly enforced, InfoSec policies are at best suggestive to most employees, and violations rarely catch anyone's attention or interest. Isn't all of this considered as tone from the top?

Over the years, these three facts have formed the environment in which most of us work. Your job is to change that environment. That is the focus of this book. The simple seven-step process I present in this book is the best way to do that. But before I do, let's delve deeper into these three facts.

Fact 1: Nobody Really Cares

So, fact number one is that most of us work in companies where *nobody* really cares about InfoSec. Now, don't get upset until you hear me out. I know we live in an age when every week another breach is in the news, and the leadership at your company will often ask you if "we're safe." But let's look at the data we have from our own companies and see if my claim isn't true, or mostly true.

If you've been in the industry for any length of time, you've likely already gathered data on the companies where you've worked. So with that data, answer this question: can you identify one executive with any clout who gives much time or thought to InfoSec? Most likely, it doesn't make their agenda. They may like to talk about it and may say they care—but if we're really being honest, and we measure their level of interest and support by their actions and the resources sent your way—then clearly, their level of concern is low.

Note

I want to identify an exception to my claim to those who work in the financial services industry, or any other *highly* regulated industry for which the cost of a breach would lead to loss of public trust that translates into loss of revenue and/or stock price. But for the rest of us, I'm going to stick by my guns and argue that nobody really cares about InfoSec, because we don't contribute to the bottom line.

Still disagree with fact number one? Then look at your last security incident and ask yourself this: what did the post-incident remediation look like? Did money and resources flow your way? Did anyone demand that it not happen again? Was anybody fired? Did any leader in the company ask for an executive summary of the events? Were you required to make a presentation to executive leadership about what happened? Did any system owners involved in the incident get reprimanded? Were there any consequences at all? Did the organization suddenly get religion on patching and updating software? Were more system administrators told to send logs to your monitoring service? Did any teams invite you to their staff meeting to discuss the root cause and ways to avoid it going forward?

Your answers to these questions provide you with a clear message on your company's culture and attitude toward InfoSec. Now what do you think? Does anybody care?

Maybe the post-incident activities were all positive at your workplace, and your company took corrective actions. Money flowed your way. Heads rolled. You were given time on the executive agenda to explain what happened. System owners were reprimanded. And executives made statements that this can't happen again. If that is your operating environment, I'm happy for you. Consider yourself lucky.

But for the vast majority of us, based on my experience talking with many of you, we don't see those post-incident activities happening often. Instead, incidents are quickly forgotten, nobody shows much interest in the root cause, and *nobody* is ever disciplined or let go for mismanaging the security of company systems or data. It just doesn't happen.

Do you need more evidence that nobody *really* cares? Look at your board presentations. Do they get pushed to the end of the day? After waiting for hours to present, have you been told that the meeting is running late, and that there's no need for a cybersecurity update? Or better yet, while you're walking into the room to give your presentation, has someone asked if your 15 minutes can be compressed to 5 since they're running late? Sound familiar?

This is our world as InfoSec leaders. You're at most a check in the box. You and your team are insurance for the company. The one throat that company leaders can choke, the fall guy if they need one. They can point to your team and say, "See? We care. We have a security team." But in the end and underlying it all, *nobody* really cares.

Suffice it to say that this "nobody cares" attitude is one of the realities you'll have to come to grips with. Get to acceptance quickly. To move forward, you must factor in the reality that you're on your own. Understanding this mindset and your operating environment will help you value the simplicity of the seven steps laid out for you in this book.

Fact 2: Nobody Understands

The second fact is that not one person in the entire organization really understands your job. That's right. No one knows the ins and outs of your position and can appreciate the diversity of demands placed on you. Many people know portions of your job or can talk about various sections of the eight domains, but *nobody* understands or appreciates the totality of the work you do. If they did, you'd get more respect, wouldn't report to the person you do, and would get paid much more.

Since no one understands your job, no one can appreciate what it takes to get your job done. Some may claim to, but in reality they don't—and you know they don't. I've worked with bosses who've told me they used to run InfoSec functions at other companies, but after talking with them for a couple of minutes, it's clear they don't know the job either. One of the rocket scientists I had the pleasure of working for (or with) didn't know the difference between logging and scanning. Ouch.

Nobody knows the diversity of services you provide across the company or appreciates the breadth of technologies you must master. For each department and team in the company, you provide a different service. For the legal department, you provide computer forensic support (among many other activities). To other departments, you write company policy, support compliance efforts, and provide business-to-business (B2B) risk-assessment services, web app pentesting, red team exercises, incident response services, tabletop exercises for simulated incidents, awareness training for general staff, and on and on. There isn't one person beyond your team who understands the diversity of tasks that make up your job description, or the demands this places on you and your team. After all, we hire "high-speed" technical people, and none of them want anything to do with running phishing tests; it isn't sexy work engineers want to do.

A Day in the Life of an InfoSec Manager

I attend a lot of meetings in the course of my day. I rarely have any free time in my calendar. However, I look at my peers in the company and observe the luxury they have of sitting in their offices for hours upon hours. I can see their calendars that reflect so much free time. I dream of a day like that, or even an afternoon with some quiet time. This is not the security leader's lot in life. We're not that fortunate. Here's a typical day at work. I think you can relate:

8–9 a.m.
Meet with one of the software engineering teams to discuss customer data flows throughout the cloud commerce systems.

9–10 a.m.
Meet with a system administrator team to discuss the need to audit the organization's domain controllers and other authenticating systems.

10–11 a.m.
Meet with the HR team to discuss the InfoSec team's involvement in the offboarding process: the use of data loss prevention (DLP) tools, disabling access to departing staff members, preserving data for those on litigation hold, deciding which systems will be placed on legal hold, indicating how departing staff members can retrieve their personal files (which you never supported) from their computers after they're gone, wiping systems to ensure no loss of data, deciding when systems can be placed back into service after legal hold, determining how and when to terminate access for departing staff members. Of course, all these processes change for every country of the world!

11 a.m.–12 p.m.
Meet with the product team to discuss the requirements for Internet of Things (IoT) security in the next version of the company's product. The product team really doesn't want to meet with you,

nor to include security requirements in the next design—no surprises!

12–1 p.m.

Risk assessment of third-party vendors. Here's a fun topic. Who's going to evaluate all our third-party vendors for information technology (IT) security risks? (This should have been done when we entered into a contract with the third party, but we didn't do it then. Now leadership is asking about our risk exposure. You get the idea.)

1–2 p.m.

Update the code-of-conduct document with the legal department. (Sigh.)

2–3 p.m.

Present the results of the latest security audit to company leadership, done under the watchful eye of the corporate audit department, and utilizing an external firm.

3–4 p.m.

Review your board-of-directors slide deck with your boss.

4–5 p.m.

Meet with the network services team to review hardening standards as well as the results of the most recent network scans.

5–6 p.m.

You finally make it back to your office, tired from a day of meetings, only to be greeted by the more than a hundred emails you got that day from staff members who need something from you…

If you're an InfoSec leader, I'm sure your calendar looks similar. And it looks like this every day of the week. I've never had a quiet period in my entire career. The demands are always there, and they never let up. As the company grows in awareness of InfoSec, it requires more services from you. There is no rest for us. I've often equated InfoSec to hockey: it's fast and full contact, and you don't ever get off the ice. You better be ready and know what you're doing. If not, you'll get bodychecked and lose your job.

Deloitte once had a chart that I love. It decomposed the 8 domains of InfoSec into 176 areas. The chart could barely fit on a standard office wall. When you looked through the chart, it didn't take long to realize that the job of a security leader spans way beyond anything provided by anyone else in the company, and the sad part of that equation is that *no one* has a grasp on the job's breadth. If they did, they might care more. (Nah, who am I kidding!)

Fact 3: Fear Drives Our Industry

The third and final fact that provides context for our work environment is that *fear* drives our industry. Consider one of the underlying assumptions we as Info-Sec leaders subscribe to: the ever-present belief that bad things are about to happen. If our network isn't being hacked at this very moment, hackers are at least acquiring the information they need to do so. We begin to worry that every new form of cybercrime is being directed against our systems. And, of course, the vendors trumpet this tune whenever they get in front of you.

Fear has driven our practices, empowered our vendors, and kept many Info-Sec managers from responding rationally to the real threats in our environment. This culture of fear has created baseline expectations that have little to do with real InfoSec. Meeting these expectations, these all-or-nothing-based standards, consumes a huge percentage of our time and budgets.

As anyone in the business of selling security knows, financial success is directly related to the level of fear held by the consumer. What security vendor could sell solutions if the cyber world was a safe place? They couldn't, so they crank up the volume on the fear message.

Why are educated, successful people spending millions of dollars on security equipment? The answer is fear. They've swallowed the fear pill, which equates to spending on security devices for their homes, cars, pets, and families. Fear sells. And InfoSec is no exception.

It's no surprise that our fears and assumptions have led InfoSec departments to continually upgrade to the latest and greatest in security technology. But vendors are not vested in our success. Their success depends on how inse-cure we feel about our security capabilities and how much we believe their products will give us what we're told we lack.

As a result of the industry's continual fear message, we can be seduced into believing we need more technology to protect the company. We've been con-vinced that not only do we need more technology, but we need the latest technol-ogy to be truly safe. Security tools are expensive, so we ask for more money. More tools require more staff to support them, or at least look at them, so we request more staff.

Over time, we've lost our way. Our decision making has been warped, and soon we have a security architecture of tools that's embarrassing. Our tools are mostly standalone and "best in class." Few integrate with any other tools without integration from your team. Our architecture is overly complex and often doesn't make sense, failing to address the true threats to our companies. No wonder we have a hundred vendors knocking on our doors every day to sell us more stuff we're told we need.

Note

The irony in all our purchases is that despite investing countless dollars in the latest and greatest technologies, the average social engineer can gain access to our systems with three well-crafted phishing emails. Ouch! And oddly enough, not many vendors are knocking on your door to help in that area. Why? Because there isn't much money in it, as it requires training of our end users. I'll discuss this more in Chapter 7.

So this is your operating environment: nobody cares, nobody understands, and fear is the underlying force driving the industry and many of your decisions. What should you conclude?

Conclusion 1: It's All Up to You

If you agree with the three facts that shape our operating environment, here's one of the conclusions we can make: it's all up to you. To be successful and protect the company's information assets, you'll have to do it alone. That's right: it's just you and your team. You most likely don't have an executive sponsor. Sorry. To get the job done, you're going to have to lace up your shoes, get out of your office, walk the streets, and knock on doors. I equate your work to that of a door-to-door missionary who hopes to get invited in, except in your case you won't have a buddy standing next to you.

Over the years, I've developed a great set of operating principles that help me and my team navigate the unchartered waters of building a program. One of my operating principles is "go where you're wanted." If anyone opens the door and invites you in, work with them until the cows come home. But if they gently close the door or even give you the "invisible middle finger," as many do, then make a note of it. Don't hold it against them, because you'll be back knocking on their door again.

I don't mean to be overly pessimistic. So please forgive me if I come across that way. I'm just sharing my observations and experience as an InfoSec leader for 25+ years. The success of your InfoSec program will largely rest on your shoulders. You're on your own. However, there is hope, as the rest of the chapters of this book explain.

Conclusion 2: You'll Always Be Under-Resourced

Since nobody really cares about InfoSec, and nobody understands your job, how can you expect to receive adequate resources for the task at hand? It's just not going to happen. This conclusion shouldn't come as a surprise. It makes sense.

Who among us is adequately resourced? We're chronically underfunded. If this isn't your situation, once again, good for you. But the rest of us live in a continual state of financial deprivation, with only momentary periods of money to spend.

Given that we are perpetually underfunded, the next question we must address is, how do we operate on a limited budget? This is where my seven simple steps come in. The beauty of the process is that it requires little funding or resources to execute. As I'll show you, you can get through most of the steps without the need for much in terms of resources. It's one of the beautiful attributes of the plan: you can get a lot of work done without any resources at all.

Conclusion 3: Being Successful Requires Thoughtful Work

I believe many InfoSec types approach their work with an all-or-nothing mentality: anything less than complete security is a compromise that's equivalent to cutting a deal with the devil. I disagree with this approach, and believe that we as security professionals should view our jobs in terms of "laps around the track," with the aim of each lap to leave the environment a little more secure than it was before you started that lap.

I've been accused of being inconsistent in my approach to InfoSec, accused of leaving it for others to deal with, and not standing up and demanding that certain security controls be implemented. But when you don't have strong executive sponsorship, you have to play a finesse game to get the job done. To move security forward without strong leadership endorsement, you have to approach your role in the company as a consultant whom others can choose to ignore or partner with. You have to approach your work in increments; a security model that achieves basic "locks on the door" is a vast improvement from what existed previously if that was nothing.

Unfortunately, our thoughts about what constitutes "good" InfoSec has been shaped by the technology industry. We've come to believe that most InfoSec problems are solved through *technology*. This has led to an InfoSec culture totally focused on cutting-edge tools that we're told will fix our problems and address the latest threats we face. As a result, many InfoSec professionals build their strategies around these technologies that make up our industry, while totally overlooking the more important side of *educating others* in the company.

Do your best to buck this trend. After all, I'm claiming in this book that the *art* side—the people side—of our work is just as important (if not more important) than the science side. So your strategy needs to be much more than a list of tools purchased to address the supposed threats you face. If the people side is more important and valuable to you in protecting the company's information assets, your strategy will have to contain a plan to get all company employees involved and doing their part to secure the company's information assets.

Your strategy should answer two basic questions:

1. How do I show the company that its investment in InfoSec is producing the return it should?

2. Are the company's information assets more secure this year than last? If so, how do I show this to company leadership?

I've put these questions to hundreds of chief information security officers (CISOs) and gotten an equal number of responses. Nobody has given me simple metrics to measure our progress. One of my intentions in this book is to do just that (Chapter 10 discusses metrics). To be successful over the long haul, you have to step back and take an honest look at what we all blindly agree to be "best practices." And perhaps challenge them.

Conclusion

InfoSec is more art than science. It requires right-brain thought among left-brain engineers, and this can be problematic for many individuals in our space. Since you're on your own to secure the company's assets, you have to get creative and find ways to achieve this.

If you view your security work as laps around the track, you'll understand the benefits of incremental improvements that come through the long, hard work of building relationships, staying close to clients, staying humble, and maintaining a spirit of service. Equipped with these, you can't go wrong; you'll be embraced by the company, and will find yourself and your department hugely successful.

The seven-step plan I lay out starting in Chapter 2 does not gain momentum or authority from fear. It's based on years of analysis and refinement. I've spent countless hours analyzing our work, questioning the industry's assumptions, evaluating alternatives, talking with industry experts, and reading our literature. I challenge our industry's so-called best practices, and I've written this book to teach you a better way and hopefully spare you from a lot of grief in the process.

My approach doesn't make sense to people steeped in industry standards. It doesn't fit their mental model or, quite frankly, their egos. I'm not writing this book to encourage the status quo. I'm writing this book to show you a better way and to encourage you to get out of the arms race of technology. If you give it a chance, you'll find my plan is simple, makes sense, and most importantly, it works.

For you to get on board with my simple process, I suggest you consider the truth of our operating environment and be willing to step back from your biases and be open to another way. I'm not here to help you live up to industry-imposed standards. Those who developed those standards don't live and work at your company. Nor am I here to help you get a pat on the back from other CISOs.

No, the kudos you're going to get will come from the employees of your company who no longer see your department as their watchdog. It will come from higher-ups who appreciate that you've balanced risk with the needs of the business. It will come from all your IT colleagues who no longer feel like they're at war with you. But mostly, it will come from knowing you've protected your company's assets to the extent they need protection, that you run a department not by fear, but by rational, informed decision making.

The examples and stories I share throughout this book are all from my own experiences. I've witnessed the transformation in security over and over in several companies, starting at ground zero and in some cases starting with a crater in the ground left by my predecessor. (You know these types, the Genghis Khans of security leaders. Our industry is rife with them.)

If you're willing to try my approach, you too can transform your InfoSec department into a well-regarded and highly valued business partner in your company. The difficult part will be letting go of your old models and approaches to InfoSec. I believe the job of every InfoSec group is to influence the company's culture and move it toward greater degrees of security, provided your business needs a secure environment. I've built my approach to InfoSec over 25 years of security leadership, and the steps I'll take you through are the ones I still use to this day. If you follow my methodology, you will totally change the way your company secures its assets. It's almost enough to give any CISO or InfoSec manager a good night's sleep.

2

The Science of Our Business: The Eight Domains

I grew up during the time period when the security landscape was covered by the *10 domains*. I've chosen to discuss our industry in terms of these domains (although now there are only eight) as opposed to one of the industry's well-known frameworks because the two are fundamentally different models. The eight domains by and large discuss the theory and science of our field. The many industry frameworks—including those from the National Institute of Standards and Technology (NIST), International Organization for Standardization (ISO), Cloud Security Alliance (CSA), and Center for Internet Security (CIS)— discuss the numerous security controls to be implemented to protect systems and data. The eight domains provide a discussion on the content of the science of InfoSec.

My intent in this book is not to rehash the content of the eight domains, but to merely highlight those sections that I believe you'll want to focus on when building an InfoSec program. Not all domains are of equal importance when you follow my seven-step process. Knowing which ones to focus on will help you build your program.

As a refresher, the eight domains of InfoSec are as follows:[1]

---

1 The eight domains were developed by the International Information System Security Certification Consortium, or (ISC)[2] (*https://www.isc2.org*). For more details, see "The 8 CISSP Domains Explained" (*https://oreil.ly/fShwS*) by Luke Irwin at the IT Governance UK Blog.

1. Security and Risk Management

2. Asset Security

3. Security Engineering and Architecture

4. Communications and Network Security

5. Identity and Access Management

6. Security Assessment and Testing

7. Security Operations

8. Software Development Security

Why Am I Commenting on the Eight Domains?

I view the eight domains as the science of our profession, the "left brain" of our work. These domains provide the technical specifics of the broad field of InfoSec.

When viewed in detail, the eight domains reveal how vast the InfoSec discipline really is. To the newbie trying to break into the field, they can be overwhelming. To the audit professional trying to transition into InfoSec, it's a wide chasm to pass, and few can make a successful transition. To those of us who have been in the industry for a while, it's remarkable how much information the security professional needs to absorb relating to our technology, processes, frameworks, and models. I don't know of another technology area with the same breadth of content.

As an InfoSec leader, you're required to have expertise in all eight domains. The 8 domains can be decomposed into more than 170 subdomains. That's right, 170+ subdomains. I recommend that every InfoSec worker be a lifelong student of our trade and master all eight domains. As I say this, I know from my own experience that it is extremely difficult to locate and hire eight-domain team members. And when you require an engineering degree, it's virtually impossible.

I argue that few have mastered the eight domains. Many in our industry specialize in certain domains and have little exposure to the others. I attribute this to the way InfoSec departments are run and the failure of many managers and leaders to encourage cross-training and professional development.

Note

Talent is hard to find, and developing a standard set of interview questions is a good idea for you and your team. Here's one that I love to ask: "Describe the difference between encryption, compression, and encoding." Responses are quite entertaining, with creativity you can't imagine. Candidate responses are often so outrageous it can be hard to keep a straight face. One candidate, when responding to a question about the relationship between bandwidth and throughput, pontificated about the new "10-bit byte" Ouch! There's much I could say about this, but not in this chapter. (I cover this more in Chapter 9.)

For those who wish to master the eight domains, the SANS Institute (*https://www.sans.org*) is probably your best place to start. Stephen Northcutt and the team at SANS have built a world-class education center for our profession. For free, you can get high-quality training courses on YouTube. I recommend that you take advantage of the many learning opportunities available and commit yourself to a career of learning.

The eight domains are the bedrock of our profession. If after reading this book you decide to follow my seven-step process, you should know that not all domains are of equal importance when establishing your program. Some are best handed off entirely to IT, while others can be sliced up so pieces are transferred to IT or engineering teams. The remainder of this chapter discusses the domains and how each should be viewed and treated in this approach.

Knowing the eight domains will give you the knowledge to traverse the technology and understand its inner workings. But mastering the eight domains will not make you successful in our field. To be effective at your job, you need to understand the art of our profession, which I've laid out for you in my seven steps. The intent of this chapter is to provide guidance on how each of the eight domains should be handled if you follow those seven steps to success. The remainder of the book, after this chapter, is dedicated to the details of following those steps.

Domain 1: Security and Risk Management

The *Security and Risk Management domain* focuses on big, foundational components of your program. Much of your time building out your program will be spent in this domain. This domain consists of the following:

- The confidentiality, integrity, and availability of information
- Security governance principles

- Compliance requirements
- Legal and regulatory issues relating to InfoSec
- IT policies and procedures
- Risk-based management concepts

This is the first and most important domain. You need to get this one right. It sets the foundation for all your future work. The activities in this domain lay the groundwork for your success as an InfoSec leader within the company and in your work with all the other domains. Although this domain covers quite a bit of material, I believe that most of your time and energy should be focused on three of the subtopics covered in this domain: IT policies and procedures, security governance principles, and risk-based management concepts, which I discuss next.

IT POLICIES AND PROCEDURES

One area you need to get right is IT policies and procedures. To get your program off the ground, your initial focus should be on three documents: the information security charter, information security policy, and security incident response plan. These three documents are the bedrock of your department and function.

Your *information security policy*, which is different from your charter, lays out the expected behaviors the company wants from its employees regarding their responsibilities for InfoSec. It sets the boundaries on security and provides guidance to all staff. You'll probably need to devote more time to this document than any other document you'll write. HR, legal, corporate audit, corporate security, IT, and engineering staff will all need to review it before it gets approved. Being thoughtful in the way you create and design this document is critical to your long-term success.

All three of these documents are covered in more detail in Chapter 6.

SECURITY GOVERNANCE PRINCIPLES

Security governance principles is the next subdomain where you should spend a lot of time during your early days on the job. *Governance* is the management of decision making. *Security governance* is the management of decisions impacting the InfoSec function. As with your IT policy, you have to get this one right too.

Early on in your tenure, you should make most of your decisions through a governance council, to allow others to weigh in on your decision-making process and to show that you are a collaborator. I recommend that you establish three

InfoSec councils from the onset to create the governance structure that guides your program going forward:

Security business council (SBC)
> The first council includes representatives from each business unit. Through this council, you'll run your entire InfoSec strategy, new purchases, security architecture, InfoSec policy, plans for awareness and education, and phishing program, to name a few.

Executive security council (ESC)
> This group consists of the most-senior people in the company. This council will review the inputs and recommendations from the SBC. The ESC will provide the final review and approval of the major recommendations arising out of the SBC.

Extended security council (XSC)
> The third council I recommend you establish consists of the most-technical people in the company. The members on this team are really an extension of the InfoSec team, and their role as advisors is highly valued. Through the XSC, you'll want to pass all the technical components of your program.

All three councils are critical to your success. They are a visible sign that your management style is open and inclusive to other departments and to their opinions, thoughts, and attitudes toward InfoSec. The frequency at which the councils meet will be dictated by the needs of the business. Whom you invite and choose to chair the meetings is also important. I always attempt to have each council cochaired by someone from outside the InfoSec team. These councils are discussed in more depth in Chapter 5.

RISK-BASED MANAGEMENT CONCEPTS

Finally, the risk-based management concepts are about understanding the company's tolerance for information loss, and then applying the security controls commensurate with that tolerance level. This isn't easy to do, let alone to get right. You need help here, and using the three councils is critical to getting risk management right. To get a grasp on your company's tolerance for information loss, ask yourself these questions: If today your company had a major breach or loss of critical data, would the most-senior people in the company care much? Would it rock your business?

I had an incident that answered these two questions for me. I experienced a breach, and it got hardly any attention. A couple of attorneys wondered whether I needed to notify our customers, but within a few days, it had all blown over as if nothing had happened. The company's response was silence. It was beautiful from my perspective. No one asked for InfoSec's opinion. No one wanted to call a meeting to understand the root cause of the breach or to ensure it didn't happen again. No incident report was submitted or lessons learned generated. It was just another event on a very long list of events, each of greater importance.

I slept so much better after this incident. Who wouldn't? This incident communicated that the company didn't really care about data breaches. I heard that message loud and clear. My job was to align with the company's tolerance for information loss (which I discuss in depth in Chapter 5), and I got the message that nobody really cared. In light of this event, I didn't need to carry with me the stress of an anticipated breach. From that day forward, I didn't. I had aligned: I would build the program the company wanted.

This incident and the company's reaction were telling for me. It provided great feedback and an understanding of the environment in which I found myself, the terrain I and my team were traversing. I learned beyond a shadow of a doubt the overall climate for risk. I could sense and feel the indifference from senior management. I understood why InfoSec was under-resourced and didn't occupy much time on anyone's agenda. This would bother many InfoSec types and cause them to take up the sword to fight the lack of prioritization of InfoSec or correct others' misunderstandings. However, instead I told my team to quickly align with the overall direction, get to acceptance, and work within the culture. I had to operate within the framework of the company's tolerance for information loss, and I did.

After the breach, I was able to revisit our policy during the next review cycle. Having the company's response fresh in our rearview mirror, I was able to calibrate much of our policy requirements. I wrote broad statements lacking details. Each policy topic was limited to just a few lines. This brevity was intentional. For example, in the section on malware, I put the statement "All company systems must have protective software" and left it at that. No more details.

As I'll discuss in Chapter 7, your path forward to increased security will be through staff education. Changing attitudes about InfoSec will be achieved only by educating the rank and file up through the executives. You don't have to accept an attitude of low importance for security. If you begin to educate staff, they will move security forward on your behalf. You'll be amazed at your results when you educate and empower system owners to take responsibility for the security of their systems. In many cases, they'll exceed the levels of security your team would have implemented.

THE OTHER AREAS IN THE FIRST DOMAIN

Though I focused on only a few elements of the first domain, I am *not* recommending you ignore the other areas. What I am recommending is that you prioritize the ones I've highlighted and that in your early tenure you place more focus on these areas. These areas are of greater importance because they provide the foundation to your program. Your InfoSec program cannot be built without these.

The remainder of the areas in the first domain (for example, confidentiality, integrity, and availability of information; compliance requirements; and legal and regulatory issues relating to InfoSec) are all important, but they don't require the same level of attention early in your program as the areas I've highlighted. As the new leader of the department, you're being closely observed as to whether you were the correct hire. You get only one chance and limited time to get the job right, so focusing on the items that matter most is critical to your early days and success.

Domain 2: Asset Security

The *Asset Security domain* focuses on protection of assets (information, software, and hardware). Much of your time building out your program will be spent in this domain. This domain consists of the following subdomains:

- The classification and ownership of information and assets
- Privacy
- Retention periods
- Data security controls
- Handling requirements

The second domain is super important, but most of its work will be done by other IT and engineering teams. Only two of these subdomains rise to hit my radar as a new leader: the classification and ownership of information and assets, and data security controls. The other three subdomains, depending on the industry in which you work, will have varying degrees of importance.

Data classification can be a lot of work, with the end game being a stratified classification of information. This is necessary in the United States Department of Defense (DoD) and other government agencies. But most likely, where you work, it's excessive. I've found it is most often more appropriate to take the company through a process (possibly utilizing the councils) in which the company's most sensitive data is identified (along with its information owner) and for each piece of sensitive data, a life-cycle map is generated to show where the data resides in your systems, from creation through destruction.

For example, customer data is super sensitive because a breach of it would result in reporting requirements to your customers. This would be a bad day for the company and no doubt impact your stock price. Therefore, the information owner of customer data should know where customer data exists, from its creation through its destruction. You would also want to paint a picture of who has access to it at its various processing and storage points. The owner of customer data (VP of ecommerce) should find this exercise valuable. The win for InfoSec is that you have the information owner (VP of ecommerce) talking with you about security controls throughout the life cycle of customer data. This is a win for all!

That's all the attention I would give to this domain except to be consulted during the decision-making process in the other areas. Of course, your team would also provide the policy guidance for the IT and engineering staff members supporting these other subdomains.

Domain 3: Security Engineering and Architecture

The *Security Engineering and Architecture domain* focuses on vulnerability management, use of encryption, physical security, and security designs in engineering work. Not much of your time will be spent in this domain in your early tenure. Many of these topics are best dealt with by your extended security team and technical leads. This domain consists of the following subdomains:

- Engineering processes using secure design principles
- Fundamental concepts of security models
- Security capabilities of information systems
- Assessing and mitigating vulnerabilities in systems
- Cryptography
- Designing and implementing physical security

This third domain is full of content that's important to any security program, but it doesn't contain topics of great concern as you start to build out your program. To begin the conversation with others in the company, I use a defense-in-depth model that's detailed in Chapter 6.

Domain 4: Communications and Network Security

The *Communications and Network Security domain* focuses on securing the network infrastructure. This is an important domain, and you'll need to spend some time on it in your first year. As in the third domain, many of these topics are best dealt with by your extended security team and technical leads. This domain consists of the following subdomains:

- Secure design principles for network architecture
- Secure network components
- Secure communication channels

Next to domain 1, this is probably the most important domain, as all your data communications will traverse over these systems, whether your infrastructure is on premises, in the cloud, or a hybrid of both. The network services team needs to be one of the IT groups you're closely partnered with. They own so much of the infrastructure upon which the business data rides.

I like to set up a monthly recurring lunch with the network team to discuss security matters and how we work going forward. This is the largest of all domains and contains most of the sexy security technologies, like intrusion detection and prevention systems, firewalls, network scanners, software-defined wide area networks, virtual private clouds, demilitarized zones, Domain Name System, web filtering tools, and virtual sandboxes. Therefore, you'll need to spend lots of time and energy on this domain.

You'll want your team members to be all over these systems as well. Ironically, firewalls are discussed in this domain, but they should be also included with access controls, and mentioned in both domains 4 and 5. You and your team will be involved in all of these subdomains. All are important and can't be ignored or handed off to others to deal with.

Domain 5: Identity and Access Management

This *Identity and Access Management domain* helps InfoSec professionals understand how to control the way users can access systems and data. It covers the following:

- Physical and logical access to assets
- Identification and authentication
- Integrating identity as a service and third-party identity services
- Authorization mechanisms
- The identity and access provisioning life cycle

I've found it best for this domain to be placed on the shoulders of the IT operations team. Your team's major contribution and influence to this domain will be through guidance in the form of policy, and auditing of credentials. Beyond the policy requirements and auditing, your team's part in this domain will be limited. This is assuming your company has a good identity and access management group.

The responsibility for compliance with the InfoSec policy falls on all the systems owners and data custodians. They will be the ones selecting the tools and designing the processes. Your hope is that someone from your team will be involved in this selection and design process, but this domain by and large falls on the shoulders of the administrators—and oh, what a beautiful thing that is. Because you all know that the management of end-user and system credentials can be a complicated world. Having the system administrators owning this space relieves you of much of the pain associated with managing it.

Domain 6: Security Assessment and Testing

The *Security Assessment and Testing domain* focuses on the design, performance, and analysis of security testing. It includes the following:

- Designing and validating assessment and test strategies
- Security control testing
- Collecting security process data
- Test outputs
- Internal and third-party security audits

This domain is once again important to you and your team. All the system audits and testing will be done by your team. You want to maintain good working relationships, so be careful how you go about testing and how you handle and report the findings.

I've found that every audit/pentest I conduct should be preceded by a letter of engagement that clearly explains the intent of the audit or assessment. This letter must clearly state the goals and objectives of the audit, the anticipated time-line, and who will receive the final report. The letter should be reviewed by the legal department, the system owner, and their manager. This gets everyone onto the same page before the assessment starts.

It is important that as the findings come in, the system owners are the first to know about them, and *not* the management of the system owner. This gives the system owner time to fix the findings, so hopefully at the project's close you can report that all findings were addressed by the system administrator.

Domain 7: Security Operations

The *Security Operations domain* focuses on security operations and is where most of your monitoring of the infrastructure takes place. Therefore, it is an important domain, and you'll need to spend some time on it in your first year. As in domain 3, many of these topics are best dealt with by your extended security team and technical leads. This domain consists of the following subdomains:

- Understanding and supporting investigations
- Requirements for investigation types
- Logging and monitoring activities
- Securing the provision of resources
- Foundational security operations concepts
- Applying resource protection techniques
- Incident management
- Disaster recovery
- Managing physical security
- Business continuity

This domain is another important area, and one that will require quite a bit of your time and energy. Most items on this list require partnerships to complete. In your first year, I suggest you spend most of your efforts on investigations, logging and monitoring, establishing some security operations presence, and incident response. The other areas, although important, can be handed off to other teams and require only limited involvement from your team.

Of all the activities your InfoSec team members will perform, *none* is more important than the work they'll do supporting the legal department on staff investigations. Of all the subareas within the eight domains, this one needs to be solid, and it needs to be owned by your department entirely. No one else should play in this space with you. Staff investigations are the sole responsibility of the InfoSec team, and no one else.

I always assign one of our best team members to investigations, especially when building the investigation from scratch. This requires an engineer with attention to detail and good people skills, because of the amount of interaction with investigators and corporate attorneys. It will take a unique individual to build this program. To develop the documentation, you'll need to establish a repeatable and defensible process that will hold up in a court of law. I don't recommend you outsource this area, as owning this area will be a lifeline to you and your team when times get tough.

If you're building a forensic capability from the ground up, send one of your team members to a SANS course to get the bible on forensic investigations and to build out this capability. There's a lot to it. If you have an unlimited budget, you can get outside consulting help. Some firms have nailed the forensic process and can help you kick-start this area. I recommend you don't keep them around, though, as you want this competency solely owned by your team.

Next to supporting the legal department with forensic investigations, incident response (IR) is another area that you and your team will want to own entirely. The IR process is super important because of the amount of visibility your team gets when the company experiences an incident. Every time an incident occurs, the spotlight will be on your team, so if you don't have seasoned incident leaders and responders, plan to send a couple of your team members to a SANS course for incident response. It will be money well spent.

Your team's role in IR will be limited to one of providing leadership (incident commander), analysis of logs, and communications. You will have to be closely partnered with the infrastructure team leads and engineering teams, as they have the right of eminent domain over their systems. Your team will most likely never touch their systems, but the system owners will look to you and your team to tell them what has happened in the environment. Your discovery from log analysis will provide this insight. I don't recommend you let the infrastructure team perform the log analysis for conflict-of-interest reasons.

Monitoring of systems is another area of focus for you. If your goal is to collect telemetry from all systems to support monitoring, you'll need all the system owners and developers to send logs to a central logging service. Good luck with this. This can take several years to fully achieve *unless* the chief information officer (CIO) is a supporter of security and directs teams to make it a priority. I've found that this is a slow road, and to maintain good working relationships, your monitoring program often functions far from its ideal state for several years.

Domain 8: Software Development Security

The *Software Development Security domain* helps security professionals understand, apply, and enforce software security. It covers the following:

- Security in the software development life cycle (SDLC)
- Security controls in development environments
- The effectiveness of software security
- Secure coding guidelines and standards

This is an important area, because most of our companies are developing software for mobile apps, cloud services, and websites. Depending on the type of business your company is in, you may develop mobile applications, ecommerce websites, cloud services, APIs, desktop software, and IoT/firmware, and you may use open source software and scripting languages to integrate systems. You will want to spend a lot of time on this domain, and have dedicated software security engineers partnered with and integrated into the development processes. Unless the leader of the software teams is a security-minded individual, this area takes much patience and many laps around the track to secure.

It can take much longer than it should to get static and dynamic testing tools integrated into the continuous integration/continuous development (CI/CD) process and have outputs being actioned by the software engineers. This is typically a tough group of people to work with, as they have unique computing needs and often view themselves as security experts in high regard.

Vulnerability and patch management is also an area of great importance. Keeping software up-to-date is one of your top concerns. Operating systems (OSs) used to be at the center of security vulnerability discussions, as we looked to the companies that made the OS patches. In recent years, vulnerability management has largely shifted to the application development space and producing secure code. It's through the SDLC or CI/CD process that InfoSec requirements are inserted and vulnerabilities are addressed. After development, my team and I have had lots of success utilizing a bug bounty program to get feedback from industry researchers who discover vulnerabilities in our software missed through the CI/CD process.

Some companies require that all new systems be certified by the InfoSec department prior to being placed into production. Theoretically, this is a great idea, but it's not agile, and updates to production code are being pushed out continually, so it doesn't make sense. The best approach is to offer the developers technical training relating to secure coding practices. I love this approach, and set aside budget to provide technical training to the engineering departments. This is another win-win. They love the courses, and we, in essence, extende our InfoSec team to those who receive the training.

Conclusion

As an InfoSec leader, you *must* know all eight domains. They are the science of our profession—the left brain, if you will, of our work. Mastering them will teach you all you need to know about the technical details of your job. However, knowing the eight domains will *not* provide you a road map of how to implement them or make them effective. This "how" side is what I like to refer to as the *art* of InfoSec, or the *last domain*.

No one discusses this last domain of our work. I believe that underappreciation of this last domain is the greatest contributor to many CISO short-lived tenures. If a CISO gets into trouble, it's usually because they were unable to navigate the many nuances of the work, as the dividing line between responsibilities among teams for security is often very blurry. Or they neglect relationships and don't get the broader support of the internal community often necessary to move initiatives forward.

To be effective as a cybersecurity professional, you need to understand the art of our profession. This last domain is laid out in seven simple steps in the remainder of this book. These steps have been developed from the many hard lessons I've learned over my 25 years in InfoSec. I've witnessed each step validated time and time again by those I've worked with.

The next chapter provides an overview of the steps. Chapters 4 through 10 then cover each of the seven steps in more detail and lay out in simple terms the road map to building a successful and sustainable InfoSec program that will allow you to enjoy a tenure beyond two years.

3

The Art of Our Business: The Seven Steps

If you've ever watched a sumo wrestling match, you've seen the collision that takes place between two very large bodies, each trying to push the other out of the ring. It's a match that always ends with a big winner and a shame-faced loser. Unfortunately, the practice of InfoSec can often be like a sumo match in many ways.

The focus of this chapter is to offer up a better way—a new way unlike the traditional sumo approach. To best explain this process, I've likened it to the martial art of judo, in which both attacker and defender roll together and end up in a different place. It's efficient, simple, and easily achieved.

I've designed my approach to building an InfoSec program as a simple, easy-to-follow, seven-step process. It has been my pocket guide for years. I've used it to develop a set of operating principles that guide my team members as they partner with the business. Before delving into my approach and the seven steps, let's look at the sumo analogy in more detail.

The Sumo Approach

InfoSec teams often use their power to try to enforce security controls throughout the company, frequently among the unwilling and uneducated. The sumo analogy is especially pertinent when others in IT or engineering oppose the InfoSec team, and the two departments begin the relentless and unseen pushing and shoving match until someone "loses."

I can't count the number of times I've heard myself or other InfoSec practitioners complain about how hard it is to improve security in the companies where we work. We complain that our IT colleagues don't want security requirements on their systems, app developers don't have the time to integrate security into their sprints, and management doesn't want to pay for it. If we do finally get a security control implemented, the end users complain about it or do their best to try to bypass it.

Nonetheless, we keep throwing our weight around like a sumo wrestler, spending time and money on the same old security projects and initiatives, while the organizations we serve receive little improvement to their security posture. Didn't Albert Einstein have something to say about this practice of doing the same thing over and over again and expecting different results? This is what it feels like when we "oppose" elements of the organization and follow the sumo approach.

The Judo Approach

Judo's philosophy is to harness your opponent's momentum to achieve a less threatening state. The aim of judo is to use your opponent's movement, to take them to a position of improvement for yourself. Judo is a martial art that does not rely merely on your own strength, but on the strength of the opponent to win the match. You want to roll *with* them. I use this analogy to illustrate that your customers have an opinion about security that is most likely different from yours, and you have to be willing to compromise to maintain relationships and to keep moving the security needle forward.

In this approach, you no longer use the sumo-style "might makes right" to force departments to conform to InfoSec policies and guidelines, but instead use the strength of relationships and others' expertise to move toward an improved position for both sides. If you're having a hard time grasping the judo analogy, perhaps it will become clearer when you read on and discover the seven steps contained in my approach:

- Step 1 is all about *relationships*—relationships at all levels of the company. Every staff member in the company is your customer, and establishing relationships with them is critical to your success. The 2020 Data Breach Investigations Report (*https://oreil.ly/8UjKo*) by Verizon shows that our customers will most likely be the ones to identify security breaches when they happen, as the InfoSec team is responsible for only about 30% of all identified breaches. In light of this data, relationships are the most important component of your program. As such, I suggest you start on them first and keep them at the top of your agenda throughout your entire tenure.

- Step 2 is what I call *alignment*. It's the process you must go through to understand the company's culture and tolerance for information loss. Knowing your company's culture and risk tolerance allows you to build the InfoSec program that the company wants—not the program you believe it should have.

- Step 3 discusses the importance of *laying the groundwork*, or what I call the *cornerstones*, of your program. These cornerstones become the architectural components of documentation, communications, technology, and governance upon which you'll build out your program.

- Step 4 highlights the need for a *communications and education program* and the importance of reaching others and educating them about their roles and responsibilities for InfoSec.

- Step 5 makes the argument that to be effective, you have to *give some of your job away*, or at least share some of it with others. The domain of InfoSec is too broad to be "owned" by a centralized department. There's just too much to do, and as I'll discuss later, to be effective, you're going to want to establish a "neighborhood watch," and get everyone involved in protecting company assets.

- Step 6 is a primer on *building your team* for maximum effectiveness. Since I assume you will always be under-resourced, you'll need team members who relish playing multiple positions—great communicators who enjoy presentations and who are also uber techies.

- And, finally, step 7 identifies those few *metrics* that really matter when building a new program or inheriting a preexisting one.

This seven-step process has been refined and well tested over many years. Whether you're building a new program or inheriting an existing one, I believe you'll find the seven steps useful as you navigate your way through your early days on the job, or use it as a comparative tool for the program you've inherited. As I stated earlier, I've referred to this process as the *art* of our profession, or the *last domain* of InfoSec.

The Seven Steps to Engage Your Organization

The formula that leads to success in InfoSec is my simple seven-step process. It will change the way you approach InfoSec, provided you are ready to challenge your assumptions of the security industry and its so-called standard practices. My process is centered on building relationships, sharing the responsibility for security with others, and not centralizing power within the InfoSec team. Each step in the process can be performed without a lot of resources other than time. The only thing you have to be willing to do is change and let go of your traditional approach to InfoSec.

The process is almost too simple to believe, but I know it works because I've lived it and refined it over many years and in several companies. It's been my road map and guide while working for several Fortune 500 companies, all of which couldn't be more different. The only thing that can hold you back from establishing real InfoSec at your organization is if "your cement is dry," and you hang onto those old InfoSec methods and assumptions. Are you ready to let go? Then read on about the road map to success.

STEP 1: CULTIVATE RELATIONSHIPS

Relationships are your greatest asset and provide your only hope for securing the company's digital assets. Forming and strengthening relationships should be the most important item on your agenda. You will be able to implement the security program that your relationships allow.

At the core of my simple process is the belief that InfoSec *cannot* be achieved without solid, collaborative, mutually respectful relationships. Your InfoSec program won't move forward if you and your team aren't constantly working to build and maintain great relationships throughout all levels of the corporation.

We all know the stereotype of the socially inept security nerd who would rather spend time in front of a computer than with an unpredictable human being. And I know that some of you readers may identify with that stereotype. That's why I've dedicated the entirety of Chapter 4 to the topic of relationships. I know for many of you this may be a showstopper. It's not the skill you've spent years developing. It doesn't differentiate you from your peers or contribute to your technical abilities. Building relationships isn't sexy engineering work, and it doesn't make sense among all the good security work you have to choose from. I get it. I understand your arguments, but hear me out and give the concept a chance.

Whatever your personality or social skills, to be successful, you'll have to focus on and build good working relationships. Without them, you and your InfoSec program will go nowhere. You'll be dead in the water. You can't be successful over the long haul, and you'll find your effectiveness as an InfoSec leader severely limited. Relationship building *is* the main ingredient for success. Relationships come first, always. And without a continual focus of keeping them central to your team's approach, the following steps will not be as effective, and you'll find you're building a suboptimized InfoSec program.

STEP 2: ENSURE ALIGNMENT

Alignment is simply about taking the time to understand the risk tolerance of your organization and then building an InfoSec program commensurate with that tolerance. Get to know your organization and align with it quickly. Culture matters. You have to find where your company's risk needle is pointed. Keep in mind that alignment changes from department to department within the company.

Accept your lot in life. Your company is most likely *not* security minded. Your colleagues don't understand your work. They don't value it or accept it to the degree you'd like. They don't design security into their products. Security doesn't make any money for the company and it doesn't occupy time on the executives' agenda. The short answer is to get over it. Don't agonize over it, deny it, or be frustrated by it. Acceptance is the first task in positioning yourself for success. It's the first part of alignment.

So, while you're building good relationships (and possibly repairing bad ones), your next step is to understand the culture of the company, which I cover in Chapter 5. Don't try to change it or demand that everyone sees things your way. Without aligning your InfoSec values with the organization's, you may find yourself trying to implement a security program that exceeds the needs and wants of your company and is inappropriate for the prevailing risk tolerance of the company's culture.

This step can be throttled based on your tenure at the company. If you've been running the InfoSec department for longer than two and a half years, I'll bet that you've probably already aligned yourself with the company's values. If you've had your job for less than three years, you may not be as aligned as you should be, and reassessing your alignment would benefit you greatly.

STEP 3: USE THE FOUR CORNERSTONES TO LAY THE GROUNDWORK FOR YOUR PROGRAM

All InfoSec programs consist of eight domains, but not all domains are of equal value, nor do all require the same amount of attention as you build your program. When building your program, you should initiate a few domains first. These areas won't require much effort to start, and the progress you make in these specific areas will set you and your program up for future success.

The four cornerstones are documentation, governance, security architecture, and communications. These four areas (which encompass many of the eight domains), along with relationships and alignment, should make up the bulk of your first-year plans.

I suggest you start with the first piece of documentation, the InfoSec charter. The charter enumerates in simple terms what the company leadership wants from the InfoSec department. It also describes the responsibilities of all IT and engineering staff and management for protecting the company's digital assets.

Foremost, the charter is a clear statement from company leadership regarding the roles and responsibilities of the InfoSec team. The primary reason a charter is so important is that it allows you to *align* with the intentions and wishes of senior management. It forces their hands to make a statement about InfoSec.

You're going to be responsible for writing it, of course, but you'll need management to sign it into effect. I've found that sitting down with senior management to explain the spirit of the charter, and the "why's" of each statement is a great way to begin the alignment process. Management's reaction to your draft will help set the course for you and your program.

To be more impactful and beneficial, your charter should go beyond highlighting the roles and responsibilities of the InfoSec team to also include the roles and responsibilities of IT management and staff. The responsibility for InfoSec does not rest solely on the shoulders of your team, and you want a charter that reflects this. Protecting the company's information assets is everyone's business. I discuss the process of writing the charter in Chapter 6. Try to get the chief executive officer (CEO), president, or chief operating officer (COO) to sign it. Once the charter is signed, it needs to be communicated broadly.

STEP 4: CREATE A COMMUNICATIONS PLAN

If you believe as I do, that your only hope to secure the company's information assets is to get *everyone* involved in the security process, then communications is your pathway. If your aim is to get the whole company involved in the security process, a communications plan is a must.

InfoSec does many good things for the company, but if nobody knows about them, you'll miss many opportunities to raise awareness. Communications is challenging to most InfoSec folks. They don't allocate time for it in their model for security. It doesn't play well to their experiences or their skill sets. Fundamentally, they doubt its value.

Many don't see communications as sexy or making a communications plan as a good use of their time. Traditional InfoSec workers will scoff at the idea, but my experience tells me that a well-thought-out communications plan that includes multiple media channels is one of the best uses of your team's time. As you practice communications activities, you'll quickly realize the time spent on communications holds the highest return on investments for you and your team.

For example, communications will make your charter impactful. Taking the charter to the various IT and engineering departments to educate them on their responsibilities will lighten your workload and enlist others in the process of securing the company's information assets. A charter is meaningless unless others know what's expected of them. But this applies to all areas of your work. The organization needs to know what security policy violations look like and how to report them. This happens through communications.

While security awareness and education lays out your company-wide security curriculum, the communications plan details all the messages to be communicated over many channels to everyone in the company. You want to take your InfoSec messages to employees. I believe communications is so important that I hire a marketing and communications person to help promote our team's activities throughout the company. One person dedicated to marketing and communications activities can connect your team's work with everyone in the company. Part of the marketing and communications efforts will be a large body of training offered to staff throughout the company. Here's where the InfoSec team has the opportunity to shine, provided your team has good working relationships with others.

The IT staff should be your closest ally, but unfortunately, it most often behaves as your toughest sumo opponent. Building relationships with the IT department and bringing them onboard through specific and relevant training will be like adding staff to your department. In fact, once you train the IT staff about InfoSec, you'll find that they often taken a stronger stand on security than you would have taken as a starting point. Chapter 7 is devoted to covering all you need to know about creating a communications plan for your company.

STEP 5: GIVE YOUR JOB AWAY

In this step, you delegate InfoSec responsibilities to others and allow them to participate in the InfoSec process. When InfoSec is done correctly, the responsibility for it is given away to the employees of the organization. Remember that to secure the company's information assets, you need everyone in the company involved. You can achieve that only if you're willing to let others in while giving much of your job away.

No longer does the InfoSec department work from within its own empire, nor is it pushing InfoSec requirements on others. The responsibilities of InfoSec rest on the entire organization as all levels of the organization will be deputized for the task. I like to call this approach the *neighborhood watch*.

Part of giving your job away is to let others outside your team in on the decision-making process. I do this by allowing the system owners to be a part of the tool-selection process. I don't buy any InfoSec tools without running them by several teams first. I allow those teams to be a part of the proof of concept, and to provide critical feedback on the viability and goodness of fit of the tools before they get added to our environment.

Finally, as you give your job away, don't be overly concerned about maintaining the responsibility for traditional security functions you believe you should. Let the charter steer you here. If the charter needs updating to reflect new shared responsibilities, don't hesitate to make the changes and let the network services team own a new security service they'd like to own. This is what you want and is evidence that you're creating the neighborhood watch, and allowing "homeowners" to protect their own "homes." Chapter 8 goes into the details of giving your job away and building your neighborhood watch.

STEP 6: BUILD YOUR TEAM

What skills are needed to build your InfoSec program? What's the profile or capabilities of the staff member you should look to hire? As you build your team, partner with the system administrator and engineers to create an "extended security team."

If you're new to your job, you're probably in one of two situations: you've either just inherited an existing InfoSec team, or you have to build one. Both have their challenges, but it's better to be able to hire your own employees and build the team you need rather than deal with the tribulations that come from an existing team of "stepchildren." If you're in the position where you assumed leadership over an existing team, you'll need to take immediate actions to set the direction for your group.

Relationships, as discussed earlier, are the *foundation* of your program, and at the heart of relationships are people skills. It will be your team members who take the messages to the masses. If they don't have great people skills, their value to you and the program decreases.

You're going to be sending them out into the client areas, and if they're unable to act in a professional manner, then you're setting yourself up for failure. Why do I emphasize personal skills so much? Because your team members represent InfoSec to about five to seven groups within the company. If your team members don't have the agility to skillfully handle this on their own, it will come back to haunt you in a big way.

One final thought about building your team. Your "extended" InfoSec team will consist of many engineers who don't work for you directly but have taken an interest in security and have become security advocates or ambassadors in their areas. These individuals are important to your success, and you want to treat them as special. I've often found that some of the greatest accomplishments for security came from others outside my team. These individuals should be recognized and rewarded in a major way. I go out of my way to do so. I must confess, though, finding techies with outstanding people skills is difficult. Chapter 9 focuses on how to organize and build your team.

STEP 7: MEASURE WHAT MATTERS

If you implement the six steps laid out so far, your organization will become a true, self-defending organism. As it matures, you'll want to measure your progress toward the goal of achieving the neighborhood watch and getting everyone involved. But as you mature and go down this path, what metrics do you use to track your progress? As you know, our industry has hundreds of security metrics to choose from. They're all good metrics. But which ones *really* matter?

I believe the *key measurement* for your success lies in a simple metric: can your employees identify a security threat or policy violation when they detect it, *and* do they know how to report it? That's it. I've used this metric for years, and it resonates with organizational leadership. It's simple to understand and aligns with the industry data as well. This metric is easy to measure and totally makes sense. Tracking this metric will indicate your progress toward protecting the company's information assets and establishing the neighborhood watch.

The next metric I track relates to phishing emails. Staff members often make a wrong assumption about InfoSec: that someone else is doing it for them. Nothing could be further from the truth when it comes to phishing emails. If staff members don't catch them, you're a goner. Phishing should have a special place in your program. Its ability to educate and shape the culture can't be ignored. The phishing program, if done properly, will educate end users about InfoSec, heighten their awareness of other security matters, and generally draw them into your world.

If over the last 15 years you've tracked metrics for our industry, you've noticed that the stats for phishing haven't changed much. As an industry, we should be shocked by the number of breaches traced back to a phishing email.

For years, it has hovered over 90%, and only in the last few years did it fall into the 80s. That's right. As an industry, we haven't made much progress in defending against phishing emails.

Considering these statistics, I suggest you keep staff education of phishing a top priority. Maybe someday we'll crack the code on phishing, but the numbers don't seem to indicate that's likely to happen. One last thought: if malicious foreign entities or other hacking organizations phish your organization every day, why wouldn't you prioritize this practice? Your staff's ability to defend against phishing emails is a key metric to monitor. My metrics for improvement are discussed at length in Chapter 10.

Conclusion

I believe the job of every InfoSec group is to influence the company's culture and move it toward greater security, as the company allows you to do so. The steps I've enumerated in this chapter to build and/or maintain an InfoSec program are the ones I still use to this day. My ideas are simple, *and* they work. In the following chapters, I discuss each of the seven steps in detail, and share examples and stories from my experiences. I believe you'll be able to identify with them.

Building a program following my simple seven-step process requires that you honestly examine many of your long-held beliefs around InfoSec and a willingness to let go of some old and possibly bad habits, receive honest feedback from the organization, and require that your team change its approach.

Most importantly, you'll have to define *success* in new terms, and this will be hard for most. Success will be measured by the overall awareness of the organization and how it functions as a *self-defending* unit. I have often referred to the leaders of InfoSec as "self-defense" instructors because they're about teaching others about the science of InfoSec and ways they can defend their systems and data. If you follow my plan, you will change the way your company secures its assets.

Stay focused on these steps, and you'll build a program that will have a legacy long after you leave. If you can separate yourself from your normal approach to InfoSec and consider the seven simple steps, you and your organization can make a huge leap forward in reducing the attack surface of your environment without buying a single piece of hardware or software.

When you've implemented my plan, you will be able to cut your staff size and budget dramatically. And most importantly, you will know your company is more secure this year than last. I believe all these steps will do more for increasing the security of your information assets than any tool or increase in head count can do.

4

Step 1: Cultivate Relationships

Now that you've had a peek at the seven steps to building an InfoSec program, I want to dive into the details of each step. Step 1 focuses on building good working relationships. Keep in mind that relationships, although the focus of this step, are at the core of each of the seven steps. As you move through each step, your effectiveness will largely result from a continual focus on relationships.

As you start to work through the steps, I suggest you adopt the mindset to put others and their interests above your own. This may seem counterintuitive and career ending, but it's not. It's about playing "long ball" and understanding that others will embrace security to the extent you honor and respect them as colleagues. I've said it many times and will say it again here: your job begins and ends with relationships.

For every brick I lay building the InfoSec program, I want the names of others etched into them. I want to give others credit as much as possible. I don't need my name on any of them. Amplify the contributions of others. Diminish your own. This is the beginning of good working relationships.

Focusing on relationships isn't about giving up control, or selling out the program or the company. Quite the contrary. You're in a way recruiting and quietly deputizing others into your "extended security team." They don't realize it, but you are. You're aligning your actions with your belief that the only way to secure the company's information assets is to have everyone involved and doing their part. Without others involved, you don't stand a chance. As I've said, I call this the *neighborhood watch*, and it all begins and ends with relationships.

Caution: The Nature of Our Work

Every InfoSec leader must be careful about how they go about executing their duties. I've learned over the years that it's not only the work that InfoSec does, but how we go about doing it, that can create friction between our team and others.

InfoSec, by the very nature of its work, discovers "stuff" that is often incriminating to someone in IT or engineering. The findings often shed light on someone's failure to do their job properly.

When InfoSec gets its hands on information of this nature, it must be handled delicately. If not, InfoSec can be put in the position of "professional finger-pointing." When this happens, InfoSec bears the responsibility for professionally shaming other groups, and possibly creating a foe for life. Be careful. Nothing will cause more damage to your working relationships than to expose the poor security practices of your colleagues.

Take, for example, what happens when our InfoSec team scans the network for vulnerabilities. Although this is valuable information for the security of the organization, the way we present the findings will make or break our relationship with the network services team. Usually, the InfoSec team reports its findings to the network services team and its leadership. The findings are received and viewed by the network services team as "bad news," and a subtle and quietly antagonistic relationship has been planted. The findings expose the fact, in front of network services management, that the network engineers aren't maintaining their systems in accordance with company security policy.

You talk about a way to endear yourself with other teams. Try this a couple of times. You'll quickly find you have no friends at all.

It's a vicious cycle. System owners will refer to the scanning procedure conducted by InfoSec as "friendly fire," and view the InfoSec team as threatening their professional capabilities. InfoSec team members, on the other hand, are just trying to do their job and secure company assets.

To solve this situation, I suggest that your team administer the vulnerability management service but require, through policy, that the system owners (in this case, network services) scan their own systems and do with the results as they see appropriate. I suggest you and your team get out of the business of scanning other people's systems and code, except during a time of crisis, such as a security incident. Let the system owners have full control over managing the vulnerabilities impacting their systems. As the service owner, you can always see their progress via the tool you administer.

Get out of the business of bringing forth data on other teams. It can only lead to tension and animosity. And it's not good for building solid working relationships.

I've seen the all-too-familiar scenario of InfoSec team members working in an atmosphere of animosity with others in the organization, especially their IT and engineering brethren, *because* the InfoSec team failed to keep relationships as the top priority of its agenda. When this happens, the organization begins to develop "antibodies" against the InfoSec team, and if the trend isn't quickly dealt with, your days can be numbered.

Most, if not all, InfoSec teams carry out their duties with the best of intentions. But it's the nature of our work and the way we go about delivering our findings that often sets us up for failure. I've referred to our positions as "radiologists" since we see everything happening in our environment, and it is our job to hold up the x-ray for the patient to see their "state of health." Our job produces the x-ray, and we should offer an opinion or recommendation if asked to do so. When I bring the x-ray forward and present it, I provide the patient with good data and let them decide how they want to respond to what the x-ray shows. Usually it shows that someone hasn't done their job properly, and if you're not careful, you run the risk of alienating a colleague forever.

The InfoSec team operates in this natural conundrum: being the group that should help the company protect its most valuable assets while also being the group that sees everything happening "on the wire." Harmony between InfoSec and its client groups in IT and engineering can be elusive, especially if you don't keep relationships a top priority for you and your team.

Creating a foundation of solid relationships is at the core of achieving real InfoSec. Without good working relationships, none of the other steps for building a security program will be effective, and most will be next to impossible to achieve. Relationships centered on listening and valuing the contributions of others will reap security rewards beyond any investment in technology or staff. In fact, establishing and maintaining good working relationships, whatever the cost, is the most important achievement that a security group can accomplish. Without them, you're doomed to failure. You may for a while run under "the cover" of your executive, but without these relationships, a reckoning will come.

Making Relationships a Top Priority

Among the InfoSec teams I've managed, I always maintain a team goal that we spend 25% of our time devoted to activities that establish and maintain good working relationships. That's right, 25% of our time. It's that important to me, and the payoff is that great.

I make it a habit to meet with the other InfoSec teams in my local business area over hosted two-hour lunches. I invite the CISO and their direct reports to meet and discuss leading practices. We do this to learn from others and compare our program against theirs. We seldom meet other teams that give much time to building relationships. These InfoSec teams from other companies assume that their colleagues share their views on security. My experience is that others don't. For this reason, we formalize relationship building, and place it at the top of our priority list and staff goals each year. I *cannot overemphasize* the importance of making relationships the bedrock of your security group.

Over the years, some of my team members have initially resisted placing so much emphasis on relationship building. They argue it's a waste of time and takes them away from the meaningful work of InfoSec engineering. Their experience and education taught them that security was the result of deploying good technologies, and not hosting lunches.

I've heard all the excuses over the years, but none hold up in the court of reason and experience. It doesn't take long for the complaining to subside. Staff members who stick around for a few months see the benefits almost immediately. The arguments against relationship building stop quickly, and it becomes a self-propagating process as team members sell its value to other team members.

Today, no one I work with questions its value. Everyone sees it as a top priority. In fact, I could probably leave it off staff members' goals, and the team members would still perform the relationship-building activities out of habit. It's also interesting that the senior people on the team realize that good working relationships make their jobs and the jobs of others on the team much easier. Relationships are that important, and they've become part of our team's DNA.

Your Program Will Be Only as Good as Your Relationships

Relationships are birthed and matured by spending time with people. I've learned that no one will willingly move in the direction of security without being led to do so. To move the organization toward improved security, the InfoSec team must take the initiative and connect with other teams. As a result of this focus, don't be surprised if you have 30 to 45 recurring meetings with individuals or groups across the company. This is a good practice.

These meetings vary in content and frequency, but they provide a forum for ongoing communication and security education. Almost always, our introductory meeting is over lunch, and typically limited to 10 to 12 people. If the group is much larger, you lose the intimacy you need to get to know people. We always have opening questions teed up as icebreakers to get the conversation started. However, rule number one for this first meeting is that we're not allowed to initiate anything about security unless they do. We stick with the "just get to know them" approach.

One of the groups we meet with regularly is the legal team. So much of Info-Sec's work supports the legal team that rarely does a week go by that we don't come together. Staff investigations, for example, are often a topic. We present the status of our current findings and allow them to ask questions about our forensic activities. This involves dialogue about next steps and what can be done in the investigation. These meetings don't always stay on the topic of investigations, but inevitably will shift to other security topics.

In our relationship with the legal team members, we've often gone beyond our normal services to make them aware of what our department can do to remedy certain situations they confront. For example, the attorneys were told by their IT support team that severance packages were stored in a "secure location" so that only a handful of attorneys could read them. After learning this, we offered to verify that this was, in fact, the case. With their approval, we crawled some network file shares, and voila, we emailed them some of the recently issued severance packages. All in cleartext. Needless to say, the files were simply in a hidden file share, with no password protections or encryption. The attorneys were shocked at our findings.

The good news was that our team offered solutions that were an easy remedy to their situation. Letting departments know where their vulnerabilities lie and what your team can do to help can be tricky. But if you're not on a witch hunt, and bring the issues up collaboratively and respectfully, then you're almost always guaranteed to succeed. In my experience, the prior relationships I developed through my meetings made the process go smoothly in these cases. And it takes only a couple of these types of events for your customer groups to become valuable supporters of your team's efforts.

Relationships Aren't Sexy

One of the difficulties InfoSec leaders face in prioritizing the value of relationships is that, among security types, relationships just aren't as sexy as engineering work. No one is talking about relationships at conferences. Understanding social interactions isn't the work that draws IT security people into their fields, or techies into the IT field.

Building relationships involves connecting with people where they're at, establishing a working rapport, and finding common ground. It means understanding the workload of the people you serve and being sensitive to their concerns around the systems and data they support and protect. This is not the work that comes naturally to someone who has spent their education and career immersed in understanding technology. So as you look to add people to your team, it would help to have people skills at the top of the list.

Hiring Staff with Relationships in Mind

Ask yourself: how highly does your InfoSec team value relationships? When you think about the kind of candidates you hire, what characteristics do you look for? I screen for very technical candidates with engineering degrees. That being said, a close second is interpersonal skills. I look for people who are self-aware and express an understanding of the value of good working relationships. I value these skills more than any certification, accomplishment, experience, or credential that illustrates a candidate's ability as an engineer.

Some time ago, I noticed that all our interview efforts targeted technically competent candidates. These candidates were passionate about securing systems and believed that security was doing a great service for the company. But many of the candidates lacked good interpersonal skills. Communication and interpersonal skills weren't on the list of requirements for the position. This was an oversight. We needed team members with the ability to communicate well, and who would value maintaining good working relationships while they worked through the issues of solving security problems.

My belief was solidified time and again when I saw friction between my team and other teams. Differences and disputes over InfoSec solutions that end in ill feelings aren't worth the price of good relationships. Avoid them.

Often the security requirements placed on projects are too difficult for the project team to implement, or there are too many to fit into the project timeline. The security requirements can involve technologies and processes that IT people are unfamiliar with, which can often leave an IT professional feeling threatened or with a belief that their project will be late. Without the relational skills to navigate this exchange, our InfoSec staff began what seemed like an endless pushing and shoving match. Our staff needed to be willing to compromise on their demands for security while building an environment of trust and mutual respect.

After all, the sky is not falling, most systems are not being "owned," and data isn't walking out the door the way the security technology vendors would lead you to believe.

I suggest avoiding a contentious environment at all costs. Its price is far too high and will debilitate any healthy organization. Once relationships have been ruined, they're difficult to restore. Once respect is lost and animosity seeps in, the inevitable downhill cycle sets in. This cycle is hard to break and is the beginning of the end for most InfoSec leaders. The seven-step process for building an InfoSec program is based upon relationships.

Building Strong Relationships: It Takes a Plan

Building strong working relationships doesn't come easy. It doesn't happen naturally and requires deliberate steps to achieve, especially because most members of your team are probably a bit asocial. Good working relationships take a long time to cultivate, so when you get started, don't assume that one lap around the relationship track will get you in top physical shape. It's a marathon, not a race. Stay the course. Apply pressure to your team to stay with it. If they elect not to, then they've opted out. They've made the choice to not be a part of something new.

I suggest you get started with weekly lunches with other technology groups. These are cheap and easy, and food provides a great setting for casual conversations. Try to keep the gatherings to fewer than 15 people. Don't set an agenda. Allow for introductions and everyone to share their favorite movie, Netflix series, hobby, or weekend activity they enjoy. By the time the second person shares, others will be chiming in, and now you're off.

Once this happens, the meeting will take on a whole new life. If the meeting comes around the table and reaches you, the leader, I suggest you share your favorite Netflix series as well, but also take a moment to highlight some of the dumb things you and the team have done. Be transparent. We're all human and prone to mistakes, so be the first to admit that and watch how others will follow.

Don't stop at lunches. I've taken groups bowling over lunch or to movies after lunch. Getting people away from work to get to know each other will go a long way to building bridges between your team and other departments.

Understanding the Value of Listening

In meetings you have with other groups, it's important that you and your staff listen first. I try to hire good communicators and then coach them on the value of listening to others. To be a good communicator, you must be a good listener.

I approach most of our meetings with the intent of not saying much, and preferably nothing at all. In fact, I've found that just showing up to a meeting makes others in the room think about security more than they would have otherwise. Many times when I've participated in meetings, someone will look down the table at me and say to the group, "Oh yeah, we also have to think about the security of this system." And I haven't said a word.

It's important that you model good listening skills and conversation practices for your staff—simple things, such as never interrupt and never complete another's sentence. Let others talk as long as they want. Ask a lot of questions and listen to the answers. Listen to staff members' suggested solutions. Try to understand. Everyone wants to be respected, so respect their contributions. Don't be a know-it-all.

It's also important to remember that most of us work among people who are just like us: they long to be valued, to be accepted, and to be validated by their contribution at work. No one wakes up in the morning and looks in the mirror and says, "I think I'll go to work today and screw everything up." Quite the contrary—everyone wants to be successful. A little patience and kindness goes a long way. Try listening first before you speak. You'll be amazed at how it works.

Reaping the Benefits of Relationships: Teamwork

One of the outcomes of building strong relationships among the InfoSec staff and other IT staff is the sense of teamwork it provides. No longer is InfoSec the department everyone despises or fears. If you keep relationships at the core of your program, by the time you work through the steps I've outlined, your InfoSec department will have the reputation for being a collaborative partner and a team others can trust. The benefits that come from being a team player will be surprising.

Nowhere was this more telling than the process I followed for our first penetration test (pentest). Typically, these exercises can be equated to an attack on the network services team. That team owns the network, and one portion of the pentest is focused on discovering the vulnerabilities in these systems. Knowing this, the network services team waits in fearful anticipation of the findings, often delivered in front of their management.

If you follow the normal process, the process considered a best practice, it's a no-win game for everyone. The InfoSec team delivers "bad" news in the form of the assessment findings. Because the performance of the network services team is scrutinized, that team finds itself in a defensive mode. After surviving the assessment/audit, they spend a good deal of time plotting their retaliation against the InfoSec team. At a minimum, they certainly aren't going to cooperate with InfoSec going forward.

To avoid this situation, I decided to conduct a pentest that kept relationship building as its central focus, above the actual results of the test itself. If you build good relationships early on, you'll find that future pentests are performed by the network services team in a manner more aggressive than I ever would have imagined. So on this first test, I decided we would turn over the findings to the network services team as they were discovered, and not wait until the end of the audit and present them in a public forum. I also decided that the assessment process would be done in collaboration with the network services team, from the creation of the statement of work (SoW) through to final report and presentation.

At every step in the process, the network services team was at the table participating in the decisions and daily updates. Nothing took place in the audit that the team wasn't a part of. The outcome of approaching the audit in this fashion was that most of the findings were remediated before the final report was issued. When the final results were presented to management, it was little more than a formality, and the InfoSec team was all too happy to report that the network services team had already remediated *all of the findings*. Win-win.

My goal was to make that final presentation good news, by making sure it did not contain any unremediated findings. The report needed to reflect the discoveries, and the fact that the network services team immediately worked to fix any exposures that were found. I believed this process would create a win for everyone.

When we tried it, it was hugely successful. The CIO even noticed the change. When the final report was delivered, not one single finding was in need of remediation. The network services team members were ecstatic as well. We hadn't thrown mud on their faces, and they wondered what kind of evil we must be plotting to have let this audit opportunity go. But there was no evil intent, just a desire to do the right thing, improve the security of the environment, and build relationships in the process.

One of the unintended outcomes of following this process surfaced the next time we conducted a pentest. The network services team learned that we had limited the audit findings to only one high-risk item, and asked that we perform a more comprehensive look. Not a bad turnaround.

We still follow this protocol for our pentests today. And what makes it so successful is that we keep relationships at the core of the process. We conduct the test as if we were members of the network services team, doing to them what we'd want done to us. We also have to keep in mind that there will be many more pentests and interactions with the network services teams.

Contention won't foster the relationships needed to work together and will be counterproductive to getting the work done. An InfoSec department that values and pursues relationships in all its work gains trust from other departments by the value and respect it extends to its colleagues.

As you will learn in the next chapter, security is never about implementing security controls that meet our expectations. Let's be honest: most groups will fall short of the level of security you and your team would like to see. The victory for the company is that today they're implementing their own security controls. Hopefully, tomorrow they'll revisit them and increase their security posture.

We strive for incremental progress, while supporting the business. We invest in relationships because, ultimately, we need to rely on others to implement security controls on the systems they maintain and manage. My advice to you is to quit being the bad guy in your company, the feared colleague whom people give in to because they are terrified of what you might do. Instead, be the person others trust and value, the righthand person with the savvy and skills to make others look good as they move security forward. Ultimately, you will be acknowledged and valued for what you add to the company.

Fostering Special Relationships

The last items I'll cover are special relationships your team will have with other groups outside IT and engineering, including legal, corporate audit, corporate security, and HR groups. These departments often have interactions with your InfoSec group that are not purely about protecting information assets. When these relationships are built on mutual respect and an interest in providing value to the company, these customer groups can become lifelines for your InfoSec team when things get tough. They'll be the ones most vocal about your value.

Let's face it: few IT groups will ever sing your praises openly. They don't operate like that, and it's not in their interest, they believe, to do so. If you're honest about it, most security folks are much more technical than their IT counterparts. Our jobs require that we have the ability to go "anywhere" within the company. So continue to sing the praises of others who contribute to and make improvements in security. You'll find you enjoy long-lasting relationships with those who traditionally were fearful of working with InfoSec.

LEGAL

The corporate group that becomes the strongest defender and supporter of the InfoSec team is most often the legal department. Many times over the years, our InfoSec team has done the computer detective work to support the legal department's litigation efforts. Computer forensics are part of the InfoSec resume. But how thoroughly and how quickly the information is received and how useful it is can make all the difference for their case. Make sure this support function is done timely and flawlessly.

We had a case that involved a staff lawsuit in which the employee had sued the company for several million dollars in damages. The case floundered, and the rumor was we were on the verge of losing. One of our team members who wasn't involved in the case jumped in to help. As they did more digging and playing with the technologies, it became apparent that our forensic work hadn't been quite what it should have been. We found that the systems in question *did* keep sufficient logs of their activity but we had evidence that the employee *hadn't* connected to the network as often as they claimed. Slowly the attorneys assigned to the case became more encouraged, and more time was given to us to dig deeper into the systems and log analysis to re-create events involving this staff member. After a few more days, and many hours of log analysis, it was evident that this ex-staff member had fabricated their entire claim. They *weren't* terminated wrongfully, and the company won the case. The amount of political capital that came our way was tremendous.

CORPORATE AUDIT

The corporate audit team is another group where good relationships can help to further the InfoSec program within the company. If leveraged effectively, the audit team can be useful to your cause of protecting information assets, and for targeting those systems that lag from a security perspective. If the relationship with the audit department is poor, the InfoSec process itself suffers, and the company as a whole loses.

One of my predecessors used the audit department as a stick, wielding it to promote their own interests and obtain more resources, control, and power. There's a reason they aren't isn't with the company anymore. This is not the proper relationship. Nor is it a good idea to use the audit staff to beat your fellow

IT teammates. In my relational model of InfoSec, I continually develop my relationships with customer groups by meeting, listening, and providing what they need to be effective in the work they do, all in the hope of inserting a little more security within their processes.

Most IT auditors don't know that much about InfoSec. They're auditors first and usually have limited knowledge of the InfoSec space, other than what they've gleaned from an ISACA website. Even those who have worked in IT previously have a working knowledge of IT that is rudimentary at best. The good ones acknowledge this.

Throughout my years, I've met only one IT auditor who knew how to work with InfoSec. Before the annual audit plan was finalized, they would make it a habit to ask me to identify those areas of IT to be audited in the coming year. This gave our team the opportunity to steer the auditor toward areas of IT that weren't pulling their weight with regards to security controls. I found this to be hugely beneficial for the InfoSec process, because the audit department has special powers to influence people and change.

If you ever get to this type of relationship with the corporate audit team, you've arrived. I write more about the audit team in Chapter 12, as I focus on an audit gone wrong, run the wrong way, with the wrong focus. In these cases, an audit tends to do more harm than good and can be a complete waste of time.

CORPORATE SECURITY

Corporate security is another customer group that can pay big dividends for InfoSec. Prior police officers or ex-military types often lead this group. They usually own some systems that control the badge systems, or the surveillance cameras around the facilities. Sometimes corporate investigations are managed from this group. So, they often rely on the computer forensic capabilities that lie within the InfoSec team. An InfoSec team would be wise to ensure that this relationship is sound. These folks tend to be vocal for good or bad.

If the support they get from the InfoSec team is lousy, they'll let everyone know. If it's good, they'll be equally vocal advocates as well. So, treat this group well. Make sure they get all they need. I'd even devote some of your staff to this group so that when the need arrives, resources are standing by.

HUMAN RESOURCES

Human resources is another internal client that should be kept close. This is usually a large group across the company. I've found that one way to build the relationship is through staff presentations. Good dialogue between HR and your team will spring from presenting good data useful to the HR team members. They have difficult jobs.

Assisting them with navigating the InfoSec rules and how they apply to staff members can be a big help to them. For example, when does use of the internet become a policy violation? How much use of corporate email for personal reasons is excessive? What are the risks of instant messenger tools? When does the equipment provided for home office use get used in ways that are a violation of policy? What are the steps to be taken for the staff member who continually fails our phishing tests? This information can be helpful to them, and your group benefits as well. A well-trained HR person is worth their weight in gold.

One activity I found to be extremely useful with all these special groups was something I modeled after ESPN's SportsCenter "Did You Know" segment. I would invite members from these various groups to join me for lunch, and during the lunch I'd present the latest end-user trends in computing and their associated risks. So items like the use of Slack by staff members, trends in Facebook, malicious use of iPhones, web-based email, and the Dark Net would be topics for presentation and discussion. The first time, I was amazed at the response of those who attended. I had hoped to do it again in a few months, but they demanded we meet monthly. I wasn't sure whether the information benefited them at work, or at home with their families. In either case, I was educating my customers, and the company benefited. This was all I cared about.

Conclusion

The goal to building good working relationships is to have allies throughout the company who contribute to the InfoSec process and begin to own the security of their systems and data. If done sincerely and maintained as an annual goal on your road map, everyone wins, and you, as an InfoSec leader, will be fulfilling the purpose for which you were hired. Word will get out that you're not seeking your own praise but quietly working with others to move the needle on security. Over time, respect and value will come your way. Put the interests of others first and see if it doesn't work as I've found it does.

5

Step 2:
Ensure Alignment

The preceding chapter focused on the importance of establishing and maintaining good working relationships—step 1. This chapter discusses the need to listen and learn from those relationships in order to design the InfoSec program the company wants. You can't build a program misaligned with the values of the many people who will be your partners in securing the company's information assets. So, as you initiate and build those relationships, start to get a feel for the company's culture and attitudes toward InfoSec. Establishing this alignment is step 2.

What I Mean by Alignment

Put simply, *alignment* means being the security person your company wants you to be. Not the security person you think you should be or the security person you were at your last company. Alignment means operating in step with the company's values and beliefs toward InfoSec and being comfortable doing so.

To get aligned, you'll have to get a read on the company's culture as well as its appetite for risk and information loss. This is where those relationships come in handy. If you get this information from your colleagues, you'll have what you need to adjust your approach to InfoSec. This takes time and requires you to exercise some emotional quotient, or emotional intelligence, and finesse in dealing with others. Failure to align is often at the root of why CISOs get fired.

I've also seen many CISOs who know very little about InfoSec, but who are able to align with the company and get along with others—and they're quite successful. It's odd how simply aligning to culture and the attitudes toward InfoSec can trump security knowledge and experience.

Choosing Where to Start on Alignment

So how do you go about aligning yourself and your team's approach to InfoSec? Where do you begin? I suggest during your early tenure as you meet with people across the organization, you ask a lot of questions to get a feel for the company's attitudes toward InfoSec. The answers you receive will provide "roadside signs" pointing you in the direction of alignment.

For example, ask if the company cares about a data breach. If the responses indicate that the "company doesn't care" much about information loss, then you've been given valuable data. I once worked for a company that didn't care much about data breaches. It took me a while to align with this prevailing sentiment, but once I did, things went much better for the InfoSec team, and the company got the security team it wanted.

Another consideration is to assess the company's level of investment in InfoSec. If the company isn't investing much, InfoSec isn't a highly valued function. Ask if information or process owners are involved with the protection of their information assets. If they're not, it's an indicator that even the information owner is indifferent about information protection.

These are just a few of the types of questions whose responses will guide you into aligning with your company's tolerance for information loss. If you're able to glean responses to these simple questions and align your attitude and approach, you've begun to align yourself with what the company wants from your position.

Seeing Alignment as the Starting Point

The alignment process is the starting point for all your work. You can't write your team's charter without first aligning your approach and attitudes. You can't write a company security policy without alignment. You can't develop a road map for your security architecture without alignment. And you can't craft security awareness and training messages without understanding the company's attitude about InfoSec.

It may shock you, but it has to be said: as an outcome of reading this book, your company's information assets may become less secure than they are today or less secure than you'd like them to be. Although I believe following these steps will result in making your company more secure, this book is *not* about improving the security of your company's assets. Improved security is merely the intended byproduct of this process. This book is about helping you become more effective as an InfoSec professional *in the company where you work*. And the starting point for that is alignment.

Determining Your Company's Risk Profile

A *risk profile* reflects a company's tolerance for information loss. This tolerance is determined by the tipping point at which the controllers of money start to care that information loss is impacting the bottom line. To find your company's tipping point, you need to determine your company's tolerance for data breaches that lead to information loss. This point is different at every company.

The best indicator of your company's risk profile is to consider your last breach or set of security incidents. The company's reaction to security incidents is the best source of data for determining where your risk needle is pointed. Did senior management get notified of the incident? Did the incident cause the company to invest more in the InfoSec team? Did anyone really care? Was anyone held accountable, and how so? The answers to each of these questions are indicators regarding your risk needle.

If you haven't had a data breach recently (lucky you), you can look at any recent security incident and get a pretty good read on your risk profile. Did the latest piece of malware disrupt business systems? If so, how high up the company did the post-incident report travel? Think back to an information disclosure incident: what were the consequences, and what did it cost the company in the marketplace? What level of manager cared? What was the company's follow-up response? Did more resources for InfoSec follow? Did InfoSec management have to report to senior management on the root cause and steps to remediate the incident? Answers to these types of questions will help you determine your company's position on the risk profile scale.

While various industries inherently have different risk profiles, you still should go through the alignment process so you can articulate back to the business the results of your early travels and what you heard the company told you regarding the value of InfoSec. Obviously, if you work in the financial services industry, your risk needle will no doubt lean higher than for those of us in less regulated industries.

The risks associated with losing customer account information in the financial sector are high. Therefore, we can assume that most financial institutions, and hopefully the ones where we bank, have a low to zero tolerance for information loss. These organizations must protect their information, and they should be investing in InfoSec to keep customer information safe. The InfoSec team should be front and center in the financial services industry. In fact, it's quite possible that the InfoSec function is run by a business leader, not necessarily an InfoSec technologist.

All InfoSec professionals must understand their company's risk profile. Knowing your company's overall risk profile and unique departmental profiles allows you to align and calibrate your approach to InfoSec. Honestly, there are departments in the company whom I rarely meet with or speak to. They don't have any sensitive information, and therefore don't need much time or help from the InfoSec team.

What if you go down the alignment path and find your company has a risk profile of 3 on a scale of 0–10? If today all of your HR data was released on the internet, it might be predictable that the C-level executives just shrug their shoulders and dismiss the entire incident. Would that surprise you? Knowing your company's risk profile means that it shouldn't. Alignment keeps you from being surprised by the response of the company, since they will have already told you of the importance of your function and the value of the information you are protecting.

The Ideal Alignment

I was introduced to InfoSec as a young US Navy officer. The Navy's InfoSec training and education was best in class. In my first assignment, one of my many responsibilities included managing a Honeywell DPS-6 mainframe. With it came a division of 25 sailors specially trained to support the system. When I started the job, I had no idea what I was doing. My only option was to learn quickly and to trust the team.

During my time on the job, my biggest education was not about the technical workings of the mainframe. Instead, it was about leadership and management, and how people tick—what kind of incentives and respect people need to perform, what motivates them, what people want from their jobs and their bosses. I'm still learning these things, and every day I see how complex people are and how their differences make every management situation unique and challenging.

Looking back, I've come to understand that my InfoSec jobs in the Navy were really easy. That's right. Easy. They were easy because there was absolute alignment within the entire organization about the value of our information and the need to protect it. Up and down the chain of command, everyone understood and agreed. No one questioned the need to protect our systems or data. No one needed convincing. I didn't have to sell it to anyone or ask for more money. The entire culture lived and breathed security. No one had to be taught its value because everyone understood the cost and risk of data breaches.

The Navy's culture is homogeneous and well educated with regards to Info-Sec. If you were to measure security and risk tolerance on a scale from 1 to 10, the Navy would be a solid 10. This is very different from what you find in the private sector. Few companies take security as seriously as any branch of the DoD. They don't have to. The assets they're protecting don't have the same risk profile or value. And the mission doesn't have the same level of national importance.

This reality is made clear in the DoD's data classification system. In this classification system, all information is assigned various levels of sensitivity based on the risk of loss and the impact that loss would have to national security. The data classification schema is well thought out and represents years of work by bright people. For each classification level, certain security measures must be followed to protect the various levels of sensitive data. Different levels even have their own dedicated networks, often air-gapped from other classification levels. Top Secret information, for example, if released or disclosed, is said to have grave implications to national security.

In this type of system and culture, it's easy to get support for security technologies, as the need for security controls is unquestioned and seen as a matter of national defense. The Navy, like the rest of the DoD, has a risk profile pegged at a 10. The entire DoD considers InfoSec of utmost importance, and aligning yourself to this approach is pretty easy.

But corporate America is a long way from the Navy. And your company will likely hold a vastly different view than the DoD when it comes to InfoSec. No doubt your company doesn't come anywhere near a 10 on the risk profile scale. And this is where the work of alignment comes into play: finding exactly where your company's risk needle is pointing. This work is going to require "left brain" muscles and *not* the technical side we all prefer to live in.

Understanding Your Company's Unique Risk Profile

I learned many valuable lessons during my transition from the Navy to corporate America. One of those lessons was that InfoSec was usually a back-office function, and the last of the system requirements to be considered. It's only been in the last 10 years or so, as a result of all the high-profile breaches across corporate America, that InfoSec has been given any consideration. Unfortunately, some of this new attention is little more than lip service.

During my first corporate job, I was amazed at how often InfoSec was not only overlooked but flat-out rejected. Unless it related to compliance, it usually got overlooked in the name of speed or costs. Security was viewed as an unnecessary cost, an impediment to progress, and nonessential to the company.

Working in an environment with little to no support, you realize you're a team of one. This is not a good place for any CISO to be. If you find yourself in that position, you want to get aligned quickly. Aligning yourself with your company's attitude toward InfoSec will give you peace of mind (if you can accept it), and position you to build the security program your company wants from you.

Back to my first corporate InfoSec job. Wanting to get off to a good start, I thought an x-ray of the organization was the place to start, and this meant a pentest. The results would provide a picture of the effectiveness of our perimeter security controls. Running this test would provide a snapshot of the company's cybersecurity defenses and potential weaknesses within its controls. It's an x-ray of the patient, if you will, and a seemingly logical place to start for any security professional. I assumed the company leadership would value this information, and would take the appropriate action to address the results of the x-ray.

The pentest took about six weeks to complete. With the results in hand, I marched off to meet with the IT infrastructure leader. I was so excited to show them the results. Surely, they'd appreciate knowing the vulnerabilities within his systems, and what our perimeter looked like from the internet. I had no doubt they would respond favorably and gratefully to the information.

I could not have been more wrong—and naive. The manager wanted nothing to do with the findings in my report. Instead of a collaborative meeting, I was beaten up. The manager demanded to know why I had run the assessment in the first place. What was I hoping to accomplish? Why had I run the assessment without him and his team? What was my purpose? Was I out to make him look bad?

They found no value from the information and were even more concerned about who would see it. To them, it was just bad news, and I was the source of it. They flat-out told me I was not a team player and the wrong guy for the job. They said the CIO made a mistake putting me in the position and that I needed to keep the good of the company in mind.

Did I say beaten up? I felt bludgeoned. I'd chosen what I thought was a great way to ingratiate myself with my new colleagues. I wouldn't have been surprised if they needed help interpreting the findings, or if they asked for help with what their next steps should be. Instead of connecting with a partner in securing the company's assets, I was deemed an official enemy of the state. This was an example of classic misalignment.

I quickly learned I was a foreigner in a strange new land. My values toward InfoSec were so different from those of others at the company, I wondered if I'd be able to survive the job. I had a sick feeling in my stomach. Over the coming months, I would continue to learn many valuable lessons from this and other clashes throughout the company. These clashes were some of my early lessons about the critical component of alignment: Not everyone will be security minded. Everyone brings their own thoughts and biases about security to the table. Few will agree with me. Fewer will want to secure their systems or data without being prompted or told to do so by leadership.

As I licked my wounds and reflected on my new lot in life, I came to realize that most of the managers in the company shared this infrastructure leader's point of view. This person wasn't an outlier. They represented the prevailing culture. The managers in this company were cut from a different cloth than I was. Their experiences and education were different from mine. And they lived and operated in foreign waters, vastly different from the waters I'd previously sailed. This was my new reality.

These lessons helped me adjust my approach going forward. They taught me the value of alignment to the company's ethos and values. It taught me that if misaligned, like a cancer in a body, antibodies would be formed against me, and the organization would develop a resistance toward me. As a result, I learned that I can care about InfoSec only a little bit more than the company does, or these antibodies will "remove" me. Once antibodies are formed, chances are high you won't be around long.

For the first time, I realized that to be effective in securing the company's information assets, I'd have to come up with a different approach. I had to align with the company's culture and shared values toward InfoSec. I had to align to *their views* on InfoSec and abandon mine, or at least leave them in the parking lot every morning.

Although this is glaringly obvious now, it was new for me then. Security wasn't in the fabric of the company. Its value and role were different at every level of the organization. Protecting the company's information assets wasn't a shared value, and it definitely wasn't something that would help move the company forward.

I'm happy to say that once I and my team internalized the concept of alignment, and what it truly meant, we were able over the coming years to adjust our approach and take the company from a point where nobody cared, to having security a high-priority consideration. Alignment made this possible.

Creating Alignment Through Councils

When I refer to *governance*, as I introduced in Chapter 2, I'm referring to the management of decision making within InfoSec. This management is not necessarily the complete control of decision making, but using governance councils to influence and guide decision making so as to be aligned with the company.

This can be a scary concept because it implies the relinquishing of decision-making responsibilities from you and your team, to a broader constituency. This is not the case. The council will merely serve as an advisory board to weigh in on the decisions put before you and your team. The use of councils is a great way to get and stay aligned with the company.

Throughout the year, I work with three councils that meet at various frequencies to address issues confronting the company and InfoSec. Some councils meet monthly, and others meet every other month or quarterly.

SECURITY BUSINESS COUNCIL

The first council put in place should be the *SBC*, with representatives from each business unit. This council allows the business representatives to voice their concerns, wishes, thoughts on culture, and the "goodness of fit" for the InfoSec issue brought to the council. This council will also serve as your board of directors, among whom you will bounce many components of your program. Through the SBC, you'll run your entire InfoSec strategy, new purchases, your security architecture, InfoSec policy, plans for awareness and education, and your phishing program, to name a few.

A typical council agenda for the SBC might contain an item relating to phishing campaigns for the company. Ask the council to provide feedback on the following: How frequently do we phish the company? Do we target individual business units? How do we handle the chronic clickers? Is training provided to those who fail the phish? Do their managers get notified? For repeat, "unrepentant felons," do we take any actions? Do we want a pop-up training window for those who fail the phish? You get the idea. Allowing the council members to shape your programs brings your clients into your world, allows your strategy and tools to be shaped by the business, and allows you to achieve alignment in the company.

As a security type, I have my own opinions about what the phishing program should look like, but this isn't important. Instead, let the council members weigh in on the phishing program. This is alignment in action. It is also great education for the council members, who will very shortly start to own the phishing program and other items brought before them for feedback and shaping.

For the flip side of the previous example, can you imagine what kind of response you would get if your phishing program wasn't shaped by a council? You might run phishing tests that were offensive, or maybe too difficult at first, or they might contain an inappropriate pop-up training window, or you may phish the company too frequently, or focus on the wrong kinds of phishing emails, or target certain groups too frequently. These are exactly the types of decisions you want the council representatives to weigh in on and make. It's best to get the council to guide you through all these considerations and more *before* you begin to phish the company. This is a major decision for the company, and these should always have the appearance of a "committee stamp" on them.

EXTENDED SECURITY COUNCIL

The second council I recommend you establish is one consisting of the most technical people in the company. I like to call this the *Extended security council* (*XSC*). The members of this council are chosen because they are recognized as the technical leads in their areas. To this council, I bring the most difficult security topics, which I call the "tasty topics," and include issues like these: Does zero trust extend to the data transfer between two entities after both ends have authenticated? Should all end users be allowed to be administrators of their workstations? If not, should anyone? If some, who?

Through the XSC, you will run all the technical components of your program. I recommend before each council meeting you meet with the most influential and technical council members—who are hopefully also the most vocal at the meetings—to run your agenda by them.

For example, this council will decide yes or no to local administrator privileges for end users, whether all systems must be hardened before placed into operations, whether security risk reviews or vulnerability scans are done before systems are deployed, whether to use two-factor authentication, and more. Discuss the outcomes you'd like to achieve at the next council meeting with these highly technical council members, and ask for their help in the discussions. You'll find you quickly have an advocate for the topic so that when the topic is raised at the council meeting, these individuals will chime in and lead the discussion for you.

EXECUTIVE SECURITY COUNCIL

Another council that should be the bedrock of your program is the *Executive security council (ESC)*. This council consists of the most-senior people from each department (willing to participate) in the company. I don't always get the executive or senior vice president from every department, but usually each department will assign one of the VPs to attend and speak on its behalf. I've found that over time, and as the security function grows in the company, the most-senior members do eventually attend.

The ESC is presented the finished products or decisions that arise from one of the other working councils. For example, this council would get a presentation on the company's phishing program—including the phishing metrics: The company average failure rate per phish. The time, usually in seconds, of the first responders. How the company's scores compare to industry averages. The number of our incidents that originated from a phish, and the implications of phishing to, say, data breaches and ransomware.

Other examples of finished decisions might be an understanding of how the company would handle a breach through customer notifications. I would present an overview of our IR process, the role of the legal team, the HR team, our communications team, and external counsel if we had to tap them for customer notifications. I let the ESC know that we've run multiple tabletop exercises with technical teams and with the managers all the way through breach notification so that we could get comfortable with everyone's role in the process. I also use this council to preview any board presentations. The council meets four to six times per year, and I suggest meeting individually with each council member as the need dictates, but at a minimum quarterly.

If done well, the ESC will also provide you with a sufficient tone from the top to signal to others that InfoSec is important and to be taken seriously. I recommend that after every council meeting, you publish the decisions to the broader IT and engineering departments. This will close the loop on your decision-making process and set the tone for the next SBC meeting.

All of these councils allow you and your team to get in step with the company. I always take the InfoSec department's strategic road map through several of these councils. This ensures that we get broad feedback on our plans, and allows the stakeholders to weigh in on our initiatives. When it's time to present the InfoSec plan for the year, I will bring some of the council members with me to present the InfoSec road map to my management. The importance of councils can't be overemphasized.

Getting Aligned the Hard Way: A Data Breach at a Financial Services Company

I had a colleague who worked for a major financial services firm where a laptop was lost with customer data stored on it. We don't know the particulars of the loss, but it was reported that the laptop was not encrypted. This was a bad day for the company. It lost billions in market share. It lost more in customer confidence.

If the laptop had been encrypted, this would have been a nonissue, with no need to report it to their customers. But somewhere within the history of management's decision-making process, the decision was made to *not* encrypt laptops. Yikes.

I'm sure this financial firm discussed laptop encryption, its merits versus its costs. I also know that every security type in the industry wants end points encrypted. But somehow, someone ignored the recommendation of the InfoSec team and decided that encryption wasn't worth it. Maybe it was too expensive. Perhaps the cost/benefit analysis didn't tip the scale. Whatever the reasons, I was told this firm moved its security needle from a 3 to a 9 in a day, which is a tough way to learn a lesson like this.

On the day of the incident, while the news was reporting the story, senior leaders were posted at exits to the buildings to verify that laptops were encrypted before they left the premises. Upper-level management was personally involved in the security of their systems and data from that day forward. InfoSec was elevated within the organization and routinely put on the strategic agenda. The CISO was moved out from under the CIO.

This type of incident-led alignment is not the preferred path. It often proves career limiting for the CISO. It also comes with a lot of finger-pointing about past failures leading up to the incident, and assignment of blame. No CISO survives this type of incident and lives to brag about it. Forced alignment is never a good thing. So I urge you to get on the alignment process as early as possible in your tenure.

Recognizing Signs of Misalignment

Since the events of 9/11 in 2001, we've seen an increased focus on security in general. This has helped to promote InfoSec in many industries, but others still have a way to go. Only in the last five to seven years, as weekly news reports have announced yet another data breach, have companies responded with greater investments in InfoSec. All the media attention given to personal privacy and to the compromise of credit cards and other financial information has been our best ally in terms of upping the value for securing information assets. And, of course, the general public's concern for protecting their personal information has increased now that it affects their pocketbooks and privacy.

The changes have been good for our industry and for the companies in which we work. Most companies have been victimized by information loss, whether by insiders or corporate espionage. As companies place more value on InfoSec, their risk needle on the security spectrum moves to the right, toward greater security. And your value goes up as a security leader.

Nothing represents misalignment more than when a CISO is the persona non grata around the company, shoving personal views on InfoSec down the unwilling throats of an organization. I hear about this far too often; for example, an InfoSec team that can't wait for the audit department to blast someone because they didn't want to listen to InfoSec. Using the audit department as a tool to beat up other departments is a sure sign of InfoSec misalignment. If the InfoSec team reports to IT, it stands with the IT staff members during an audit. They're one team. The results reflect on the performance of the department as a whole.

Other signs of misalignment can be found by looking at your InfoSec group. Ask yourself these questions: Has this group been moved several times? Have there been multiple changes to the leadership over the past few years? Does the group suffer from long-standing differences with other areas of the business? How often do your customers call with a complaint or a request for your services? When an InfoSec group is approaching the job aligned with the company and its culture, managers and other professionals are calling to request security assistance.

Complaints, on the other hand, are clearly a bad sign. While talking with other InfoSec professionals, I've heard stories of InfoSec personnel getting flogged while trying to do the right thing. If you're getting flogged, you're not doing the right thing! You're misaligned. So align quickly. It's possible the company doesn't want much security at all, and that's why you have only a few staff members! The messages are there, often right before your eyes. But you have to be looking to see them.

Many of us still subscribe to traditional thinking, buying wholesale into InfoSec standard operating procedures and practicing an approach that barely worked even before everyone started caring about InfoSec. The problem for many of us is that we haven't taken the time to understand what our companies really need from us. I've met few people who can articulate this. It's sad this is the case, and that most InfoSec leaders don't know how to get this information and calibrate their approach to align with the company's wishes.

If you're like most InfoSec professionals, myself included, you're naturally between a 9 and a 10 with your personal security needle. Security is in our DNA. We live and breathe it. We would never deploy a system that wasn't locked down hard. We believe all projects should address all the risks, or at least all the high risks. Our perimeter should be impenetrable. Mobile devices should have all the bells and whistles protecting the physical asset, the electronic transmissions, and the data on them.

We're so committed to security that we often battle other groups (who have to manage and support these systems) to get them to see things our way and protect the company assets. We're martyrs, believing that someday "they'll see." Someday our dire predictions will come true, our careful planning will pay off, and then everyone will recognize us as heroes and acknowledge the worth of our fights. Unfortunately, this never happens.

The CISO position has a fair amount of turnover, and that's understandable. I listen to stories all the time from InfoSec folks who are not comfortable in their jobs. Many lack the professional and interpersonal skills required to navigate the subtleties of sensitive management situations, or the relationships and communication required for managing an InfoSec department. Alignment is often the missing ingredient keeping our colleagues from being successful. Alignment is key to your success and to the company's intention for InfoSec.

If you build an InfoSec program that reflects the security values of your company, you will provide the level of protection the company wants from your team. Others won't fight you. You won't be at odds with other departments or system owners. There will be agreement and, for the most part, harmony. If you take this path, I believe that one day you will be acknowledged for the part you play in securing your company's information assets.

Please understand my message: you will never be acknowledged for your work if you have not aligned yourself with your company's risk profile. Instead, you'll be alienated. Your job will give you an ulcer. You will find yourself in daily battles with your colleagues outside the InfoSec team. Eventually, you'll suffer a martyr's death and be walked to the door.

Sound familiar? I've seen it happen far too often and to well-intended InfoSec professionals. They know their job and have all the credentials. They understand the technologies and have solid experience from good companies, but many of them are enemies to the culture and the company they work for simply because they are misaligned.

Conclusion

I tell my team members all the time to be softer on security than our colleagues. That's right. If your colleague is a 5, be just a little to the left of that. This will allow that person to own the security of their system and data. The employees will implement security after they know you're not going to demand certain standards or cram it down their throats. It may feel counterintuitive, but it's a good guide for your work. And I encourage all of my team members to live by it as well.

I view my team as backseat drivers. Our job is to whisper in the driver's ear about the risks of the situation or decisions. It's their choice whether to implement any security. It's a business decision. We're risk advisers, and nothing more, unless we're invited to be so.

Corporate America lives on revenue and profits. Unless security contributes to profits, it's just another burden on costs and part of the overhead bucket. At most companies, InfoSec is an add-on, considered at the end of everything else. And truthfully, most managers would rather not deal with security at all. Projects or processes would be much easier without having to consider InfoSec. If you're fairly new to your company, the process of alignment will go hand in hand with building your base of relationships. As you meet with others, ask for their help and coaching. Indicate that you'd like to align with the company and build the security function the company wants.

If you ever hope to secure the company's assets, align with your business partners quickly. This doesn't mean you give up your desire for a more secure company. I'm advocating that you help your company be as secure as it desires to be. Only when you align with your customers can you partner with them to protect their information assets. It's your only hope. And let this truth sink in: if you don't align with the company, it will replace you with someone who will.

6

Step 3:
Use the Four Cornerstones
to Lay the Foundation
of Your Program

Step 1 focused on the value of relationships and getting to know your organization, its people, and culture. Step 2 was a necessary process of calibrating yourself to align with the company's prevailing culture toward information security. Both steps are about getting to know others and making the internal adjustments within yourself to calibrate your approach to security, so that you can give your company the security department it wants from you.

This chapter covers the work of putting pen to paper and establishing what I like to refer to as the *cornerstones* upon which the early years of your program will be built. For steps 1, 2, and 3, you don't need to hire anyone. All this work can be done by you alone.

The Four Cornerstones

With progress being made in steps 1 and 2, you can now turn to the actual work of building your cybersecurity program. There's no time requirement for steps 1 and 2, so when you start on step 3 (the four cornerstones) will be dictated by your unique work situation. I do want to highlight that as you begin the work of the four cornerstones, you should never stop the work of building and maintaining relationships, and calibrating yourself to the company's culture.

Let's now look at these four cornerstones, the foundation of any InfoSec program:

- Documentation
- Governance structures
- Security architecture
- Communications

These four areas, along with relationships and alignment, always make up the bulk of your 30-, 60-, 90-, and 180-day plans you provide to management.

What About a Pentest?

Some of you may argue that I've omitted the obligatory pentest or risk assessment that should always take place in the early days of your tenure. I would counter this argument by positing that you don't have enough information yet to scope the pentest, and executing one at this time would do little to ingratiate yourself with your new organization. While you're trying to establish good working relationships, let's not drop that pentest "love letter" on their desks.

As you follow my seven-step process, there will come a time when an initial audit or risk assessment will make sense. But let's spare your new colleagues the heartache of doing one until your good working relationships are well established and your outlook about your job is aligned with the company's.

Cornerstone 1: Documentation

You need to put in place three documents early in your tenure to lay the groundwork for success. These three documents are the bedrock of your department and function:

- Charter
- Information security policy
- Security incident response plan (SIRP)

Putting these in place early is critical to your success. Let's take a look at each document and my recommendations for what each should contain.

THE CHARTER

Simply stated, the *charter* enumerates what company leadership wants from your InfoSec department. It lays out in clear and simple statements the responsibilities of the InfoSec team while also enumerating the *responsibilities* of the IT and engineering teams for protecting the company's information assets. The charter is important because it is a clear statement from company management regarding the roles and responsibilities of your team and how each of the eight domains is divided among you and your colleagues outside of the InfoSec team.

The charter spells out your team's purpose for being employed at the company. Having a charter in place allows you and your team to align with the intentions and wishes that senior management has for InfoSec. The charter forces their hand to make a statement about InfoSec. It will set the tone and define the boundaries of your activities.

The charter is the primary vehicle for discussing with other departments (IT and engineering) the role your team will play in the company. These discussions are invaluable to your long-term success. More importantly, while writing the charter, you allow senior managers in IT and engineering to insert their ideas and interests in InfoSec and for you to enlist them in your work.

Fundamental to any sound InfoSec program is the belief that *everyone* is responsible for information security. Protecting information assets does not rest solely on the shoulders of the InfoSec team; it is everyone's responsibility. The charter documents this shared responsibility. As the CISO, it is your job to make it everyone's business. Chapter 7 covers this topic further.

Where to begin and what to focus on

You may discover that you work for a company that doesn't care as much about InfoSec as you do. That's OK, as long as you realize it. Codifying the company's interest level and translating that interest level into your charter is what this document is all about. Deloitte has published an InfoSec chart that shows the InfoSec space comprising approximately 175 areas; knowing which ones will be your responsibility and to what degree is a main goal of the charter. Ultimately, the charter will clearly communicate to the IT and engineering departments about everyone's shared responsibilities for protecting the company's information assets. The charter is a RACI (responsible, accountable, consulted, and informed) chart (*https://oreil.ly/bHni4*) in prose form.

So where do you begin with the charter? I recommend starting with the eight domains. List them one through eight. Then next to each one, write one simple management edict or statement about what *your* team will do to support this domain. One sentence is all you need. For example, for domain 6, Security Assessment and Testing, your one statement could read something like this:

> *Conduct periodic risk assessments to ensure that the security strategy and architecture are keeping pace with technology and the changing needs of the company.*

That's all you need. This gives you and your team the responsibility for conducting audits of systems and data to ensure they are being safeguarded in accordance with the needs of the company and the capabilities of technology in the market.

Next, include a section on roles and responsibilities: one for the CIO, IT management, IT staff, engineering staff and management, and the InfoSec team. Write one or two sentences describing the responsibilities of each group. For example, here is a statement that could be included to spell out the responsibilities for IT management and staff:

> *IT management is accountable for the security of the systems data that supports their business processes. They are responsible for implementing and maintaining systems, in accordance with cybersecurity policy and standards.*

For example, if the IT department is responsible for providing video teleconferencing solutions like Zoom or Webex to facilitate virtual meetings for employees, then the IT department is responsible for the security of those systems. Likewise, if IT is responsible for providing laptops and end-user computing equipment to employees, then IT is also responsible for securing those assets throughout their life cycles.

As you develop your charter, I encourage you to keep it to one page in length.

How to pull it together

It's your responsibility to write the charter, but you'll want management and staff from across the company to be involved in its creation and approval process. To get the document reviewed, you'll have to "drag it through the streets" and solicit feedback from the many teams impacted by the document. This also means that your charter may not come back looking anything like the document you initially created. That's OK. It's part of your alignment activities. In fact, that's what you want! Appreciate the feedback and collaboration.

Before you discuss the charter with senior management, you should share it with your direct reports. Their inputs to your simple statements are critical. Your direct reports should share it with their team members for feedback as well. The only rule at this time is to do your best to keep the document as short as possible. Remember, write simple statements about each of the domains—no books and no long-winded paragraphs.

I've found that just by developing the charter collaboratively with others from across the organization, staff members start to own the security function with you. The charter (and other documentation) is one of the cornerstones of your legacy. And the beauty of the document is the process you follow to create it. Crafting the charter through conversations and meetings with others is the ultimate alignment method. During the document's development, both parties align with each other. You, as the security expert, have the opportunity to hear the thoughts and wishes of those outside security. While the general staff members are confronted with aspects of security often for the first time, that must be addressed in their daily lives.

Keep two thoughts central to the outcome of the charter development process: senior leadership participation is critical, and the role of protecting the company's information assets *must* be shared by everyone in IT and engineering. If you keep these two goals central to your efforts, the charter will be a success.

When taking the document to senior management, I've found the most beneficial way to gather their input is to first provide a copy of the charter and then visit them in person. Spending one-on-one time with each of them is key to gathering their thoughts. Not only will you get more information added to the document, but the discussion you share allows you to help shape their thoughts on security, for better alignment. You will quickly find out where management stands on security and who your advocates and detractors are.

This process also ensures they'll own the charter going forward. I've found that having these conversations equates to getting what we want out of the document while still giving credence to the ideas that came from management. Just the conversation alone leads them to believe the ideas came from them and invests them in the final document. In the end, you don't care who "owns" the ideas, as long as senior management has been part of the development. This will be critical when you and your team share it with their staff members.

You, as CISO, will have final editorial rights. My guess is that the charter ultimately won't stray too far from what you want. If the document doesn't look like what you anticipated, that's OK as well.

Meeting with the Boss

Once your document has incorporated all the thoughts and input from the meetings, the final step is to discuss it with your boss. I suggest you get an hour of your boss's time, if they can afford it. This meeting can be very telling.

It was during a charter meeting with my boss that we were able to discuss and develop our shared vision for the InfoSec program. During this conversation, I learned my boss knew more about security than anyone on his staff of three thousand. In addition, he was emphatic that to successfully protect our company's information assets, everyone had to be involved.

Furthermore, he believed that he, and only he, could make security a responsibility in everyone's job description. I couldn't have asked for a better meeting. I hardly said a word the entire time. But when we were done, we were on the same page, and I knew he supported me and my function. The charter was completed. All senior managers had a hand at crafting it, and my boss blessed it as is and signed it. Alignment was well underway.

Now comes the difficult work of communicating the charter to the organization. This could take many months to complete and requires participation of everyone on your team. With the charter as our guide, we met with each IT and engineering group to talk about security. This was our opportunity to extend the hand of collaboration further. We wanted them to know we were not there to rat anyone out, but to partner with them to move security forward. Because senior management had blessed the charter, none of what we had to say was a surprise, and our goals were mutual.

INFORMATION SECURITY POLICY

After the charter has been signed into effect, your next chore in documentation is to get an *information security policy* in place. This policy lays out the expected behaviors the company wants from its employees regarding their responsibilities for InfoSec. It sets the boundaries on security and provides guidance to all staff. You'll probably need to devote more time to this document than any other document you'll write. HR, legal, corporate audit, corporate security, IT management, and engineering staff all need to review it before it gets approved. Being thoughtful in the way you create and design this document is critical to your long-term success.

Where to begin and what to focus on

The information security policy fundamentally reflects the behaviors and actions the company desires of its staff to protect the company's systems and data. If all policy requirements were achieved, the company would attain the level of security it wants for protecting its information and computing assets. If your policy doesn't reflect this, you've got the wrong policy.

The key to getting the policy right is that it must align with the risk culture of the company. It must capture the company's intent for information security in written form. To get the policy right, you must assess where the security needle is pointed in terms of risk tolerance and then write a policy that aligns with that tolerance level.

This is not an easy process, and far too many InfoSec leaders start with a government website or industry standard. This is the wrong place to start unless it aligns with the company's appetite for information risk or is required for compliance reasons. Most industry standards (for example, ISO, NIST, and Open Web Application Security Project, or OWASP) are written assuming that the security meter is pegged at maximum security, National Security Agency style.

ISO documents have been developed collaboratively by the best minds in our industry, and the security they've built into those documents are Fort Knox certified. This is not bad, but it most likely doesn't reflect the risk tolerance of your company. The government has high standards for information security. Your company probably doesn't.

Therefore, the level of detail in your information security policy, and the requirements of the security controls, need to be carefully considered. For example, consider your password policy. Deciding its length, strength, and composition may be better left to a committee and mandated through a company-wide standard. In contrast, the policy statement for passwords may require only that all systems be protected by passwords, without specifying the requirements.

You'll also need to decide who signs the policy. As with all other company policies, I recommend this be the most senior person in the company. After all, the information security policy has just as much weight as an HR policy, or the code of conduct, or any other company policy, for that matter. The enforcement of the policy does *not* fall on the InfoSec team any more than the enforcement of company working hours falls on the HR team.

Managers must enforce all company policy. This is their job. This is to avoid situations where, for example, someone visits a website they shouldn't and the company wants the InfoSec team to police this and address the culprit. The policy should clearly state that this is the manager's responsibility, so we always pass these types of issues along to the employees' manager. Let them handle all policy violations in their area, just as they would if someone were sexually harassing another employee.

Drafting and reviewing your policy

Creating and writing the first draft of the policy is fairly easy. Reviewing it and soliciting feedback from the myriad of teams, leaders, and managers who need to review it takes several months to complete. Ultimately, when the policy finally gets presented to senior management for signing, you want to be able to say that "you dragged it through the streets" and that every IT team, engineering group, and HR leader provided feedback, similar to the way you developed your charter. This brings credibility to your process and ensures that you've aligned the policy to the company's culture and risk profile.

Finally, part of the process for maintaining the InfoSec policy is a periodic review. I recommend every six months you review and update the policy, cover to cover. This process is important, as it allows you to make adjustments to your original document and calibrate it to align with the company's risk needle. After several review cycles, you'll probably have your policy dialed in to the company's culture and attitudes toward information risk—right where you want to be.

Getting the policy published is a lot of work. For the InfoSec leader in a new organization where no information security policy exists, this will be a heavy lift. For the InfoSec leader who inherits an existing policy, I recommend you wait six months before you suggest any changes. This allows you the necessary time to learn how the organization works and understand the company's culture. If you touch the policy document too early in your tenure, you may be seen as overly aggressive, recommending policy changes in an organization that you're not that familiar with. Avoid this.

SECURITY INCIDENT RESPONSE PLAN

The final piece of documentation needed to complete this cornerstone is the SIRP. *Incident response* (IR) is the process of responding to and leading the company through an analysis of events that have put systems and data at risk by threatening the loss of confidentiality, availability, and integrity.

In this day and age, incidents are the soup du jour, so documenting this process is unavoidable. Once it's documented, you must train the organization on their roles and responsibilities. This is often best done through a tabletop exercise.

Where to begin and what to focus on

The SIRP is super important because it is used only when the company's systems and data are at risk, and all eyes are on you and your team. Given the amount of visibility your team gets when the company experiences an incident, you'll need to have well-trained incident responders on your team, able to lead during a time of chaos and uncertainty. If you don't have seasoned incident responders, plan to send a couple of your team members to a SANS course for IR training. Incident response is another area that you and your team will want to own entirely.

Your team's role in IR is one of leadership (incident commander), and analysis (of logs). You will have to be closely partnered with the IT team leads and engineering teams as they have "right of imminent domain" over their systems. Your team will most likely never touch their systems, but they will look to you and your team to tell them what has happened in the environment. Your discovery from log analysis will provide this insight. I don't recommend you let the infrastructure team be the only team to perform the log analysis, because of potential conflicts of interest.

How to write the SIRP

Obviously, you will write the first draft, but like the charter and information security policy, the SIRP document needs to be reviewed by the system owners since they will be the ones whose systems and data are the focus during an incident. The SIRP should contain a section on roles and responsibilities, as well as a flow-chart indicating how incidents are handled and who is involved at each phase. Each incident should be closed out with a lessons learned session, and a final report generated to company leadership, telling the story from root cause through steps taken to restore company systems and data.

TAKEAWAYS

Keep in mind that the completion of the documentation for the first cornerstone happens early in your tenure—say, the first six months. This is done while you're building relationships, and aligning yourself with your new employer and its tolerance for information loss. Your job is to build the InfoSec program the company wants and needs from you.

You can always turn up the dials on your program as the company becomes more educated regarding InfoSec. However, in your early tenure, allow the various groups to be involved in your decision-making processes. The outcome of those processes will produce documents that are in line with the relationships and alignment you've achieved across the company at this stage in your tenure.

Cornerstone 2: Governance

Governance was discussed in detail in Chapter 5, so I will not give it much discussion here beyond a quick review and summary. As mentioned in that chapter, *governance* is the management of decision making. *Security governance* is the management of decisions impacting the information security function.

I recommend that you open your decision making "town hall" style. This will allow others into your processes and show that you are a team player. Similar to your approach to writing documentation, letting others in on the decision-making process helps you achieve alignment with the organization. This is helpful to you as a security leader, since our natural tendency is to push for full security even if it isn't necessarily what the company desires or needs. Letting others influence your decisions can be disconcerting because it implies handing over your decision-making responsibilities to others. But trust me, it's to your benefit.

For every manager or leader, it is critically important to establish an early set of quick wins to gain momentum while building the InfoSec program. Doing so creates positive optics for you and helps others see you as a "winner." Establishing an open governance process can easily be one of those early wins.

I recommend that you establish three information security councils: the Security business council, Extended Security Council, and Executive Security Council (all covered in Chapter 5). The existence of these councils creates a governance structure that guides the establishment of your InfoSec program. Each council is made up of different sets of people from across the company (technical leads, representatives from the lines of business, and executives).

The key to all councils is to let its members weigh in and voice their thoughts and opinions. You want this. Don't get this confused with relegating your decision-making authority over the InfoSec function. It's not. You're asking for their input and guidance to allow you to make better decisions. For more details on each of the governance councils, refer to Chapter 5.

Cornerstone 3: Security Architecture

The third cornerstone is *security architecture,* or the thoughtful design of your security tools and processes. This is yet another area where you need others involved in its design and implementation. As you know, many of the security tools in the modern enterprise are managed by others outside the InfoSec department.

Security architecture can be an obscure topic for many, so I suggest you start by presenting the organization with a simple logical model focused on security controls at each layer of your computing stack: application layer, mobile and laptop devices, the network layer, servers and data centers, and cloud services—for example, Amazon Simple Storage Service (S3), virtual private cloud, and Elastic Compute Cloud (EC2) instances. If you're able to document these, highlighting any gaps in your first year, this would be great progress.

WHAT DOES ARCHITECTURE LOOK LIKE?

I like to represent the security architecture by using a simple *defense-in-depth model* (Figure 6-1). This concept is easy to grasp when represented in logical concentric circles, which also makes it easy to document all your security controls (logical, physical, and administrative) by layer or concentric circle. This simple model will resonate with both the techies and executives, and year after year it will be an easy way to measure the progress the organization is making in addressing any gaps in your security controls.

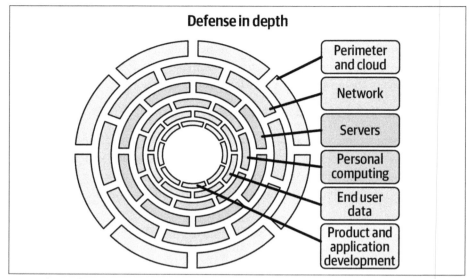

Figure 6-1. Defense-in-depth model

The defense-in-depth model starts with each concentric circle representing one layer of your company's IT infrastructure or systems architecture. The layers of your infrastructure are up to you, whether you are mostly cloud based, on premises, or a hybrid of both. Most companies will fall into the following situations: cloud systems, perimeter networks, internal networks, data center/servers, desktops, handheld devices, data, and personnel.

With the inclusion of cloud computing, the model still works, but the names of each circle will change to reflect the cloud layer and technologies like VPCs, security groups, zones, and workloads/microsegmentation. On each layer, list your current security controls. Include the technological, physical, and administrative controls.

Then you can show a picture of the threats your company faces and any gaps you have in the defense-in-depth model in addressing those threats. I know it looks simple, but that's part of its effectiveness. I've found that for most IT and engineering types, this is the first time they'll see the state of their security defenses. It's also a good idea next to each control to indicate the team responsible for that control. This will give the viewer a good picture of the role the many groups are playing in the security of company assets.

HOW TO PUT THE SECURITY ARCHITECTURE TOGETHER

To build your first security architecture, I suggest you plan meetings with each of the IT departments to introduce them to the model and the overall defense-in-depth concept. Naturally, these discussions will lead to their "concentric circle" of responsibility. For example, during your first meeting with the end-user computing team or client engineering team, you might find they have the following set of security controls in their circle: anti-malware controls, encryption of hard drives, logging, host-based intrusion detection systems (IDSs), backup processes, DLP tools, OS hardening, and vulnerability management practices.

I suggest you document their existing security controls and do so without much discussion about gaps or threats. This is their current as-is architecture. It's neither good or bad, adequate or sufficient at this time. Your goal is to get it documented and to get them talking about their current set of security controls. Save discussion of changes for future meetings.

During your next lunch meeting with the client engineering team, I suggest you share the security controls for laptops as contained in the NIST document. The NIST framework is not intended to be your standard for laptop security, but to educate the client engineering team on the variety of security controls available to them. I guarantee that by projecting this list, you'll trigger a great discussion with their thoughts on the security controls they could implement. Two meetings in, and they are already discussing security improvements.

WHAT'S THE OUTCOME OF DEVELOPING THE SECURITY ARCHITECTURE?

Taking the various IT and engineering teams through an architecture exercise has many benefits. Foremost is education. The teams will gain an understanding of the many security controls available, many of which they weren't aware of. For example, the client engineering team may discover that installing host-based IDSs will help combat the spread of malware and provide safeguards for malware missed by the anti-malware software installed. Most client engineering teams are unaware of host-based IDSs until your team informs them, often by reviewing a list of best practices for securing laptops.

Another outcome of developing a security architecture is that teams will start to think about their road maps for security and make plans to implement security controls in future iterations of the systems they support/own. For example, our client engineering team realized after their second meeting looking at best practices that they had only 5 of the top 10 security practices implemented. As a result, they placed the remaining five on their road map for the following year, presented it to leadership, and received funding for all the planned security controls. We attended those presentations and had to say very little. Instead, the client engineering team did all the talking. They sold every new security control to leadership and presented the tools and costs. It was wholesale approved on the spot.

One more advantage to having these architecture meetings with the many IT and engineering teams is that you and your team have the opportunity to ask the key question they should consider when designing their security architecture: what are the threats you face? That's the key question for the client engineering team. What are the key threats to confidentiality, integrity, and availability, and how have you taken steps to mitigate those risks?

The outcomes of this type of discussion are huge for you and the company. This leads the client engineering team to begin to think about the "why" of their work. For example, if the laptop is lost or stolen, what security controls are in place to protect the company from loss of sensitive information? The team will get to the solutions of encryption, remote wipe capabilities, strong passwords, backups, LoJack, and possibly more. This is a win for you and your team, and all you had to do was order some lunches, present some industry frameworks, and discuss best practices.

On that note, the last benefit of the security architecture exercise is that management will see that you are under-resourced for the task at hand. I've been in this position many times, and it's nice to hear management acknowledge, "InfoSec is going to need more people!" Often at this point in my early days I've been asked for a staffing model for the InfoSec organization. I find this to be the best path forward, with management admitting you need to increase your staff.

Cornerstone 4: Communications, Education, and Awareness

If you subscribe to my assertion that your only hope to protect the company's information assets is to get everyone involved, then you're going to need a communications plan. A *communications plan* will contain your strategy to reach every staff member in the company regarding their unique responsibilities for information security. Staff members won't know their responsibilities unless you tell them. They won't know their responsibilities unless you communicate what's expected from them regarding information security. It's the communications plan that makes this a reality. Communications is a never-ending process, and so important that I hire a dedicated staff member to lead our communications and education efforts.

Not many InfoSec teams will dedicate a head count to a communications person. To me, they are the most important person on the team, focused solely on communications, awareness, and education. With one staff member dedicated to this function, the rest of the team will likely for the first time consider ways to reach areas of the company that otherwise would have gone overlooked.

One of the common rules of marketing is that people have to hear something seven times to make it stick. InfoSec requires just that kind of communication—clear, concise, compelling messages repeated over and over. Chapter 7 covers the details of communications, education, and awareness.

THE BENEFITS OF TRAINING AND EDUCATING OTHERS

Part of your communications plan is training. Providing training to others is one area where the InfoSec team gets to shine. If you train the organization's IT and engineering staff through a variety of InfoSec technical training courses, you'll deputize a powerful group into the security team. The IT staff should be your closest ally in protecting the company's information assets, and providing specific and relevant training will be like adding staff to your department. In fact, I've found that once you train the IT staff about information security, you'll find them owning the security in their areas and not needing much help from your team.

Plan to spend a large percentage of your budget on awareness and training for all staff. This amount of investment is challenging to most InfoSec managers because training doesn't fit their model for security, and it doesn't play well to their experiences or their skill sets. Fundamentally, many security types doubt its value and view it as a waste of time, so suggesting they devote a large portion of the budget to this activity seems nonsensical.

However, my experience tells me that a customized training and education curriculum for administrators, general staff, managers, and executives will give you the highest ROI of your team's time. As you provide training to others, you'll quickly see results and understand the value of the training. Training of IT and engineering staff helps other teams understand your foundational documents like the charter or the information security policy. On their own, these documents don't mean much to general staff, but after you provide InfoSec training, you'll witness how these documents are taken more seriously. Training will also educate IT and engineers on the SIRP. This will be a huge lift for your team. Deputizing trained engineers in the way of IR makes incidents so much less challenging, they almost become nonevents because for those trained in the process, they become second nature.

Developing a communications strategy is key to your success. It details the messages to be delivered to everyone in the company, along with who from your team will deliver the message and the frequency. If you take communications, awareness, and training seriously, your organization will become a true, self-defending company.

All of the communications activities I've listed here, and those I discuss in Chapter 7, will do more for increasing the security of your information assets than any technology or increases in staff. While you're building relationships and aligning with the company's culture, you can start these activities immediately.

Conclusion

All security programs consist of eight domains, and over time you'll be deep into all of them. The four cornerstones I've highlighted in this chapter are where I urge you to start if you're new in your job. For those tenured in your positions, these cornerstones can also be used as a quick benchmark. Focusing on the cornerstones of documentation, governance, security architecture, and communications will set you up for success and allow you to build the security function your company wants from you. The walls of information security surround the entire organization. Implementing the four cornerstones will require lots of hustle to complete, but hopefully you enjoy building a program as opposed to just maintaining one.

7

Step 4: Use Communications to Get the Message Out

I'm a huge believer in the power that communication, education, and awareness can have in your pursuit to secure your company's information assets. Of all the activities I give my time to as a CISO, none is more important than or has the ROI of communications. If I could do only one activity in the InfoSec space, it would be this one.

This topic is so important that for over 20 years and multiple CISO gigs, I've always had a dedicated communications person supporting the team, amplifying our work, and broadcasting InfoSec messages throughout the company. If Info-Sec were a body, communications would be the heart of the program. If you're not focused on communications as a CISO, hopefully this chapter will give you some things to think about.

What Is a Communications Program?

A *communications program* (or simply *communications*) is the thoughtful delivery of targeted and relevant messages to the various departments and teams through-out the company that inform them of their responsibilities for cybersecurity. A communications program is proactive about security, and the goal is to provide information to staff that causes them to take actions toward greater measures of security over the information assets under their control. Communications is the vehicle by which staff members understand their responsibilities for safeguard-ing sensitive digital assets.

Communications encompasses awareness, education, and training. It's the many channels through which cybersecurity roles and responsibilities are communicated to staff members, and it makes educated consumers of all staff members. Since people learn through different media channels, a good communications program will consist of a variety of vehicles, each designed to reach staff with the messages they need to hear. Here's a sampling of communications channels that a well-rounded program may include:

- In-person presentations
- Cybersecurity conferences
- Lunch-and-learns for nontechnical staff
- Technical training sessions
- Raffles and giveaways at company-wide events
- Tables at company events (which give an opportunity for your team to get out and meet others and spread the word)
- Handouts like pens, with reminders on them of the importance of security
- Company-wide emails
- Phishing campaigns
- Notes from the CISO (especially effective following a company-wide incident or breaking news story)
- Posts to internal electronic bulletin boards (Facebook's Workplace, for example)
- Office/workplace posters
- Desktop notes left on staff desks
- Tabletop tents on cafeteria/coffee shop tables
- Animated or live videos
- Nonanimated cartoons
- Video games and company-wide competitions
- Cybersecurity articles on the company's portal

As a security leader, communications should consume a large portion of your time. As you can see from the variety of delivery mechanisms, having someone on your team whose job is dedicated to communications is critical. I have a creative side, so this activity really engages my interest.

Why Is a Communications Program So Important?

The best way to illustrate the importance of a communications program is by example. Imagine that you have an unlimited InfoSec budget and could purchase every tool on the market (I've known some CISOs who appear to be in this situation). Now imagine you have one staff member who receives a phishing email, clicks the link or attachment, and is successfully phished (not many tools on the market can protect against this behavior). Even with an unlimited budget and the acquisition of all those tools, it takes just one uneducated staff member to mishandle a phishing email, and boom, you've been owned.

That's the point: communications is the *best way* to inform employees about actions they can take to protect the company from potentially compromised situations. There's no other way to reach them with this information, and in many situations, *no* tool or software can protect the company. Humans are required to evaluate and respond to the situation. You can be successful in safeguarding company assets only if every employee is doing their part and knows how to recognize and report a security policy violation. For this reason, communications is one of the main pillars in my seven-step program.

A good communications program will be your opportunity to highlight the many good things the InfoSec team does for the company. Few inside the company understand the myriad of processes, groups, and functions that an InfoSec team must work with.

For example, InfoSec's role in procurement can be quite involved, but few are truly aware of our role. As each contract is awarded, the InfoSec team should be involved to ensure that the contract specifies the right terms and conditions to safeguard the company electronically. If the third-party vendor is to receive access to the company's data, how will that data be protected on their end? What will the employees of the third-party vendor be given access to, and for how long? Who will monitor their access privileges for policy violations? If data loss or theft is occurring, how will it be detected and reported? Only the InfoSec team is able to raise and resolve these issues. Communicating this throughout the company will make everyone aware that as contracts are awarded, staff members must include the InfoSec team in the process.

Communications Within the InfoSec Team

Communications are critically important to the InfoSec team because most InfoSec types aren't great self-promoters. We're engineers who like to keep our heads down and our eyes glued to our monitors. We prefer to stay focused on the technical challenges of our industry. If we have to get out of the office and give a presentation, no thanks.

Look at your team members. Most of them would probably prefer technical work to giving a presentation or training session. Most techies prefer the human-computer interface rather than standing in front of an audience of 30 unfamiliar people. It is the responsibility of the communications person to review the work of each staff member and identify opportunities to communicate this work out to the broader company. A good communications person will amplify the contributions of your staff that would have otherwise gone unnoticed.

Another tendency I've found is that InfoSec's contributions are seldom realized by others because we're often too busy, unwilling, or unmindful of the need to tell others about them. We're also tempted to believe that doing so might be perceived as "tooting our own horn." If you've hired a solid communications person, they will connect the dots here and draw this information out of the InfoSec staff. It's their job. A good communications program informs the company of the team's many positive contributions.

For example, consider the work involved to implement a software-as-a-service-based (SaaS) file transfer service. For IT, this can be delivered in about 15 minutes. IT integrates it into the company's authentication solution, makes the SaaS service available to staff, and voila, you're up and running. But to offer it in a secure fashion, the timeline is greatly expanded. The security controls to be implemented will take several meetings to discuss and decide. Understanding the sensitivity of the information the SaaS service processes, the access rights and privileges of the users, the app's ability to support two-factor authentication, if not via Security Assertion Markup Language SAML, then natively through the app/service itself, the monitoring of the apps events, and getting logs from that service into your logging and monitoring service, the testing of the API for vulnerabilities, the integration of DLP services into the API of the SaaS service, the backup and retention of data kept in the service, the ability to support legal investigations if needed, monitoring the app's use through alerts being set should someone download excessively large amounts of data—the list goes on. Communicating these considerations to the IT staff will help educate them about the myriad of services your team provides. Without a communication program, however, these types of support services are often overlooked and underappreciated by the company.

The Goal and Objectives of the Communications Program

The goal of the communications program is to inform every staff member of their unique responsibilities for maintaining InfoSec *and* how to report policy violations when they're detected. That's it. Therefore, the communications plan must include individual messages crafted for each department, team, and process owner. Obviously, the company's technical teams will be the recipients of a broader variety of messages as opposed to the general staff members working in finance, who may need to know only a few items related to the security of the data they process.

Security is everyone's responsibility. It is not the sole responsibility of the InfoSec team. This belief lies at the core of your communications program, and communicating to each and every employee is key to your efforts and success. The communications plan enables you to do this.

Some suggested steps for communicating throughout the company are as follows:

1. Identify every business unit, team, group, leader, and process owner.

2. For each entity identified in step 1, understand the sensitivity of the data supporting their business process.

3. Identify the policy requirements affecting that entity.

4. Identify the behaviors you'd like to instill in this team/individual that would enable them to protect their information.

5. Craft a message to achieve this behavior.

6. Decide how best to deliver the message. Table 7-1 shows example content over the course of a year, and Figure 7-1 shows various communications channels you can employ to deliver your message across the company.

7. Identify who on the InfoSec team will deliver which messages and to which groups/teams.

Table 7-1. Sample communications plan road map

	Feb	Mar	Apr	May	Jun	Jul	Aug	Sep	Oct	Nov	Dec
Video Newsletter	Phishing		Laptop security		MFA		Training		cybersecurity conference		Incident reporting
Roadshow Video		Phishing		MFA		Customer data		Training		WiFi	
In the News	COVID-19 as newsworthy events arise										
Lunch-and-Learn Events			Incident reporting		MFA			Training	cybersecurity conference		
Ambassador Program		Phishing	Customer data		MFA	Phishing	Passwords	Training + cybersecurity conference			
Council, All Hands	Phishing	Phishing	Passwords	Customer data	MFA	MFA	Training	Training	Training	cybersecurity conference	Training
Email		Phishing report out		Phishing report out	MFA	MFA	Phishing report out	Training + cybersecurity conference	Training + cybersecurity conference		Phishing report out
	Phishing program										
Posters, Desk Drops					MFA			Training	cybersecurity conference		
Workplace Graphics	Incident reporting	Laptop security	Passwords	Customer data	MFA	MFA	cybersecurity conference + passwords	Training	cybersecurity conference	WiFi	Phishing

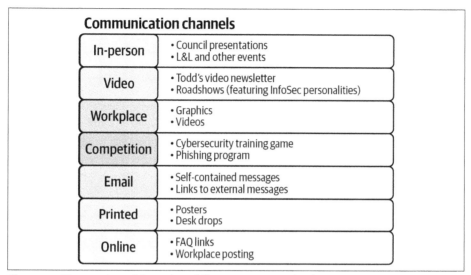

Figure 7-1. Use a variety of channels to deliver your communications messages

Starting Your Communications Program

I believe the most important team member on any cybersecurity team is your communications person. Preferably, this person is specialized in marketing and communications. If you don't have a team member dedicated to this role, I strongly recommend you consider one. I've used the same marketing and communications firm for nearly 20 years. Having worked with them for that long, they've become security experts who are able to quickly draft up materials without much involvement from me or the team.

I've found it enormously beneficial to have this person embedded as part of the InfoSec team. That role is so important that this individual owns the first portion of our weekly staff meeting. The initiatives this person tracks require visibility and participation from the team. I consider the position the most important one on the team, and I think it's important for the entire team to know that. Over time, the InfoSec team grows dependent on the communications person, and they become instrumental to all components of our work because just about everything we do requires some measure of communication.

NOT ALL DEPARTMENTS REQUIRE EQUAL LEVELS OF COMMUNICATION

The details of any communications plan will depend on the complexity of your company and its departments. Three client groups that I've found occupy a great deal of energy in the communications plan are the HR, legal, and corporate security departments. I hold regularly scheduled meetings with each of these teams. These meetings are a part of our communications plan and do more to increase awareness among these groups than anything else we could do.

In my past positions, I've established quarterly meetings titled "Did You Know" for the legal and HR departments. I use this time to educate them on the latest in internet scams, phishing attacks, instant messaging tools, social media scams, mobile apps, email, voice-over-IP (VoIP) scams, social media platforms, remote desktop tools, the Dark Net, and other relevant activities. Discussing these topics with the legal team members not only helped them understand the trends among our staff, but was also useful in their personal lives. This made their jobs easier and helped InfoSec by increasing our value and extending our team into the legal department. This regularly scheduled meeting was our opportunity to help them understand what was happening across the cybersecurity world.

At my first meeting, I had no idea of the kind of response I would get from the attendees. I discovered that many of the attorneys were eager to learn for their own personal knowledge. For example, in one meeting we discussed the Dark Net and hacker boards and how readily available hacked usernames and passwords were. The discussion quickly turned to the implications to our company and staff. And presto, we had the attorneys making decisions for greater security that would have never happened without these meetings. The result of that particular conversation led to more meetings and an expanded audience within the legal department.

News of this meeting spread to the other groups within the legal department. Soon we were meeting with the IP attorneys, discussing protection of the company's intellectual property, which led to the initiation of a data loss prevention project. This project was sponsored by the legal department and would never have occurred had it not been for the InfoSec team communicating relevant information to them. This is a clear example of how communications allowed us to connect with another department, which in turn took ownership for the security of its data and systems.

YOUR TEAM'S RESPONSIBILITIES

Communication must be a full-court press, and everyone on the InfoSec team must be involved. Your team has to "own it." Communications will require a time investment on your part if you hope to reach everyone in the company. Often this means taking the message "to the streets" yourself.

Your team owns the entire communications plan. Team members must be involved in every phase of its development, and they must be assigned to individual efforts within the program. Further, they should be incentivized in their outcomes, and as you get the message out, your team must be ready for the response you'll get and the subsequent work that will follow.

Communications at Work

Some of the examples I'm about to share could almost as easily be included in the chapter on relationships, or even alignment. So in the situations I describe, I highlight the communications component, although many other pieces could aptly apply to several others of the seven-step process.

EXAMPLE 1: TRAINING WITH INDUSTRY EXPERTS

I had tried for over a year, working with the network services team and not wanting to damage our blossoming relationship, to get IDS systems installed but was met with one excuse after another as to why it couldn't be done. No matter which network engineer I approached, the installation was stonewalled. My initial reaction was that the network engineers were up to no good and didn't want us seeing their internet traffic. My other theory was that they were incredibly lazy and allergic to work, and didn't want us seeing that.

Whatever the situation was, I couldn't make any progress. My last choice was to escalate the IDS implementation within the organization to get the work forced upon the network services team. I knew if I did this, I'd win the battle but lose the war, so I refrained from that option.

Finally, it occurred to me that I had another option: I could bring in a network security training course offered by a professional security organization. I would review the curriculum and ensure that network monitoring and IDS systems were included in the materials, and then hope for the best. I chose this path.

I made arrangements to have the class offered on site with lunch provided. Don't underestimate the power of feeding techie types. All of the network services employees were invited, and most of them showed up. During the time of the class, I was sitting in my office when, much to my surprise, one of the network engineers attending the course rushed in to thank me for the course. Without hesitation, they asked me if we had IDS systems installed at any of our internet points of presence (POPs). I responded that we did not. They were shocked and insisted we needed them. I told them it was a brilliant idea. It took me a while to pick my jaw up off the floor. The course had paid for itself before its first snack break.

Within two weeks from the completion of the course—that's right *two weeks*—we had IDS systems installed at all our internet POPs around the world. Keep in mind, I'd spent the better part of a year trying to get them installed through finesse, and by hook or by crook. One course from an external vendor, and magic! This little episode taught me a valuable lesson on technical training and on the use of industry experts to get work done.

EXAMPLE 2: COLLABORATIVE DECISION MAKING

On another occasion, I learned that the company had entered into a contract with an external vendor to host all of our email services. It was hard to argue with a decision like this, because it made sense to everyone. But what seemed like a good idea for the IT department was unacceptable to the legal department.

Because of our previous work on a myriad of issues with the legal team, the attorneys were fairly well educated in InfoSec. When they caught wind of the outsourcing idea, they met with the CIO to voice their concerns. The project was halted. Needless to say, the email administrators got InfoSec religion quick, and the CIO wanted to know why someone from our group wasn't on the project team. Ha. Good question.

The CIO knew we weren't ratting out the email project team either. They were aware of our weekly meetings with the legal department and understood we used the meetings to educate the attorneys. It was through this weekly communication that we made the legal team aware of the outsource plan, and they understood the implications of email being hosted and supported by another company.

Their adamant opposition to the deal came with the organizational clout to stop it. Without our weekly conversations, this never would have happened. The regular communication and mutual respect we built strengthened our InfoSec practices. This is precisely the kind of increased collaboration that comes from having a good communications plan, and that leads to smart decisions about InfoSec across the company.

EXAMPLE 3: INFOSEC CAMPUS EVENTS

Another company I worked for placed a high value on education and academic achievement. Because of this, I was able to sponsor a two-day security conference in our conference center on our campus. The conference was well attended from among the 3,500 IT staff. We brought in great speakers and had some of the senior IT managers speak. The CIO gave the keynote address.

Beyond hearing industry leaders speak on relevant topics, this kind of event also allowed for breakout groups to address some of the specific interests of IT staff. Those who attended were steeped in the message of security and, as a result, gained knowledge and interest in what our group was doing in the following months. In the end, the ROI of such an event was over the top, as the message of security was conveyed to hundreds of staff members, and little of it was delivered by the InfoSec team.

Signs the Communications Plan Is Working

Building a strong communications program requires focus and energy in an area not usually considered part of an engineering team's remit. But how do you know if your communications plan is working? As we communicate our security message across the company, the groups we interact with start to own the InfoSec responsibilities in their space. This, in turn, causes the demand for our services to rise. The InfoSec team will have to be ready to meet this demand and to let the requesters participate in the security process.

As the demand for our service rises, the InfoSec team adds more staff members, and your communications army grows. I found that once the communications plan was underway, the demand for our services rose so quickly we had a staffing shortage within the InfoSec team and were unable to hire fast enough. This is a vicious cycle. It also exposed the need to educate others on InfoSec so that they could address some of their own security needs without depending on our team for support.

Occasionally, I've learned the hard way about what doesn't work in the communications arena. At one company, I thought I'd have a surefire hit when we brought in the leading internet law expert to speak. It was a symposium open to the entire company, and no one showed up. What a disaster! I attributed the attorneys' lack of interest to the fact that they were already getting all the information they needed from us through my quarterly Did You Know meetings and the almost weekly meetings to discuss our forensic case load. What I do know is that not all your efforts will produce big results, but if you stay at the task, your team will see dramatic results, and in the long run the ROI of communication will be off the charts.

Conclusion

Getting the communications program off the ground begins with having a marketing and communications person on the team. The responsibility for developing the communications program will rest with this person. A successful program must have a communications plan that guides your team in a thoughtful and intentional way.

The plan must include targeted messages and the delivery mechanisms for each department and the subsequent behavior goals you hope to accomplish. The entire InfoSec team must be involved and incentivized to achieve specific goals. You'll know the program is working when demand for InfoSec services is rising and staff members are being added to the team. You'll also notice that employees are reporting more incidents, and business units are taking responsibility for the security of the information supporting their business process. Communications can be fun for those with a creative bent. I personally enjoy this part of the overall cybersecurity work, and next to relationship building, I place it at the top of the value chain.

8

Step 5:
Give Your Job Away...
It's Your Only Hope

Chapter 7 discussed the importance of communications and education to the security leader. Hopefully, you'll give some thought to the role communications plays in your organization, and the multiplicative effect it can have in your efforts to secure information assets. As you educate others in the company, and especially those in technical positions, you'll often be able to either partner with another team or completely transfer to that team a piece of the InfoSec pie.

Don't resist transferring security responsibilities to others outside your team. Although our natural tendency is to keep those responsibilities under our control, releasing them to another team is putting in place the neighborhood watch throughout the company. Remember, I said your company doesn't stand a chance unless everyone is involved in protecting its digital assets. Giving portions of your job away to other colleagues is a blessing you shouldn't pass up.

Giving Your Job Away, a History Lesson

Let's take a brief look at the history of computing since the 1990s to understand how security responsibilities have naturally transferred to other teams as our industry has matured. This transition of InfoSec responsibilities to others in the company wasn't my idea; it's been happening for a while. I just happened to spot the trend in the late '90s and have watched it accelerate since then.

The question for every security leader is, what role do you play with those teams now responsible for some portion of the security pie? To effectively "manage" these transferred processes, you need well-established governance practices, as highlighted in my discussion on security councils in Chapter 6.

THE 1990S

To those of you who were in the industry 25 years ago, you will remember that most, if not all, security activities were performed by the security team. Before browsers existed, we used search tools called Archie, Gopher, and Veronica, which crawled our directories to retrieve files we searched for. These services were first found among government agencies and universities.

I was in the Navy during this time, and all InfoSec functions were performed by dedicated security engineers and cryptographers, most of whom were DoD contractors. Electronic communications, depending on the classification level, were encrypted using encryption keys that were manually rotated at predetermined intervals. Most computer equipment was stored in secured locations called *sensitive compartmented information facilities (SCIFS)*, which were restricted vaults containing classified materials. Most of the security processes and controls were physical controls. For example, you often needed two people to enter the SCIF, and written logs were kept to record the names of individuals entering along with the date, time, and purpose of the visit. For top-secret SCIFs, each of the two people entering had a portion of the key required to unlock the door.

Later in the '90s, we were busy installing wired networks like Fiber Distributed Data Interface rings and 10-baseT Ethernet networks, and in the early '90s we were just beginning to connect these networks to the internet. With new internet connections, firewalls had to be installed, but not many were available on the market. The first firewall I used was from Trusted Information Systems, out of Rockland, Maryland, called the *Gauntlet*. The firewall was treated as the ultimate access control device and *not* managed as a network device. As such, its administration was naturally performed by members of the security team, and *not* by the network support folks.

The Gauntlet firewalls were super innovative, as they had site-to-site virtual private network (VPN) capabilities, the ability to transfer public keys over the wire, and a layer 7 proxy (no other firewall to date had this type of innovation). Prior to the Gauntlets, you had to install keys using a floppy disk (5 1/4") and coordinate the date/time of the key installation. The Gauntlets automated all this for us.

For disk encryption, we were using the NSA's Fortezza cards, which encrypted the hard drive through the Personal Computer Memory Card International Association (PCMCIA) slots. For file encryption, AT&T had a desktop package called *Secret Agent* that was a handy application allowing for file-level encryption and the ability to attach files to one of the few email systems in use, in our case, DEC's TeamLinks.

My point in mentioning these technologies is to illustrate that in the early days, all of these tools were administered exclusively by the security team. Nobody else on the IT team was allowed to touch them. We wouldn't think of letting others outside of security management have control over these systems.

THE EARLY 2000S

As we approached the early 2000s, security teams often continued to administer and manage the organization's firewalls. However, that responsibility quickly shifted to the network services team as we acknowledged that firewalls were basically networking devices (routers) with access control list (ACL) capabilities. A similar transition also took place on desktops and laptops. InfoSec teams were previously responsible for all the security controls on the end points. Technologies such as antivirus software, disk encryption, end-point firewalls, host intrusion detection, log collection, and backups all were responsibilities of the InfoSec teams.

By the mid-2000s, all of those tasks had migrated to the IT engineering teams. This transfer of security tools marked the beginning of the shift of security responsibilities from the security team to others throughout the company. Among the security departments privy to these shifts, we discovered we played more of a governance and oversight role than a hands-on administration role for these tools. The great shift was in full swing.

THE LATE 2000S

By 2010, identity management (IDM), also known as identity and access management (IAM), was one of the last functions to be transitioned out of security and into the system administration or operations team. Ownership for directory services (AD and LDAP) or Amazon Web Services Key Management Service was transitioned to the system administrators or operations team. Rarely would you find the security team performing IAM functions. Whether we liked it or not, by 2010 we found ourselves in a distributed model of security, or what I have coined the *neighborhood watch*.

In simple terms, the neighborhood watch is an operating model that makes system owners (for example, a Unix administrator or network engineer) solely responsible and accountable for the security of their systems. As in a neighborhood with limited police presence, the neighborhood watch shifts some of the responsibility for "policing" into the hands of the residents. Everyone is expected to be on the lookout for suspicious behavior, and to report crimes or suspected crimes when they're observed. This is the model for the neighborhood watch.

As this trend to give security tasks to other IT and engineering groups continues, I strongly recommend you leverage it. I believe it's your only hope to truly secure the company's digital assets. If you encounter an opportunity to transition some of your work over to other teams, give close consideration to it. You're not going to lose your job, and it only helps to further your cause as the security leader. The neighborhood watch is a great model to strive for, and it is for the overall benefit of the company.

2010 TO TODAY

Today, the security function secures an IT infrastructure that is all cloud based, and our security responsibilities look nothing like they did 25 years ago. Yes, many of the same tasks are being performed, but not by the InfoSec team. For example, the DevOps team does almost all of the security for its environment. We supply some basic enterprise identity services, and mandate the use of cloud orchestration and compliance software, but all core security functions and decisions for our cloud operating environment are performed by the DevOps team. It's through governance models, as discussed in Chapter 6, that the InfoSec team is able to provide leadership and influence.

The security of platform as a service (PaaS) is largely a responsibility of the development teams. The software security engineers who report to me have little to do with securing the development processes. We can suggest, consult, offer assistance, and try to influence, but in the end it falls on the shoulders of the developers. Welcome to the neighborhood watch! Today few security teams are involved in supporting any of those tasks beyond consulting and policy guidance. It's why I'm a big fan of RACI charts, and being very clear on roles and responsibilities for security and who is doing what.

Understanding Your Challenge

Many of our functions have transitioned to other teams, and I propose this is good for you and the company. But it does create a dilemma for you: although this transition has taken place, your company leadership still thinks you're responsible for security across the company and that you're involved in all of these areas, providing leadership. In many cases, company leadership looks to you as responsible and accountable, even though the truth is, you're not.

As I mentioned in Chapter 1, the odds are against you because nobody really knows your job. Few senior executives have any security experience. This is why I suggest you use RACI charts among all your security partners so everyone is clear regarding roles and responsibilities for security in their areas. Creating RACI charts is time-consuming, but the task is well worth the effort. Going through the process with the teams will lead to clarity around roles and responsibilities for their security tasks. This will benefit both parties and help solidify the neighborhood watch, a model I believe you want.

McAfee, You Surprised Me

I want to put in a plug here for McAfee, because it made a brilliant move: McAfee hired a prior CISO to be its CIO. What a great move by McAfee! I've been predicting this trend would happen for years.

If you look at the to-do list of most CIOs and infrastructure folks, it's a long list of security initiatives. The hardware and software in our systems is not unstable, as it was 15-20 years ago when lots of outages led to significant system downtime. Today our systems are so stable and reliable that availability is rarely an issue.

And with the advent of software as a service (SaaS) and infrastructure as a service (IaaS), there isn't much in-house work for CIOs to do anymore. Most of the development (cloud services, mobile apps) has been handed over to engineering teams. Other than business process work, CIOs have lost the core of their work to SaaS companies, which have taken the place of in-house developers.

Most CIOs I meet with now claim they have security experience—no doubt to protect their jobs. So this move by McAfee to hire a prior CISO to fill the CIO position was brilliant. Naturally, that person will be on top of all the security issues, and if they have the customer service skills required of CIOs, then it will be a great move for McAfee and its clients. I believe this trend will continue. And more current CIOs will claim they have security in their backgrounds.

Relationships and the Neighborhood Watch

As the InfoSec world has moved to this new distributed model of the neighborhood watch, the value of relationships has escalated. The new neighborhood watch asks the business and systems to share and own responsibilities that they historically never had. For example, an InfoSec team may not be that involved with the company's data sciences team and blind to where the team pulls its data from, and where the output of their analysis is stored. If this is the case, the InfoSec team will have little insight into the security controls throughout the process.

InfoSec provides some general security controls for authentication, network layer security, and encryption of data at rest, but we most likely have no idea of the security controls used throughout the data analytics process. One of the messages in the neighborhood watch is that the InfoSec team is here to help, but like the local police department, we must be called in to be of assistance. If invited in, we get as involved as the system owner would like, but until we're invited in, we're able to influence only through policy.

In the neighborhood watch model, the security team should be involved in discussions with the system owners about the many security controls possible to them as system owners. Not that you approve or review the details, but you're involved across the systems landscape with the security decisions being made. You don't want your system owners performing security functions without your involvement.

Being involved connects you back to the many cybersecurity governance councils I spoke about earlier. Through these councils, you're able to partner with your fellow neighbors (system owners) to provide the proper guidance and technical support they need in order to feel as though they have sufficiently protected their assets.

The Need for Governance

As security tasks and responsibilities get spread out among the various teams, the importance and need for governance rises. As I discussed in Chapter 6, governance is an essential way to align with the organization. In the world of the neighborhood watch, governance becomes a cornerstone of your efforts as a security leader. All of the security councils should be owned by you and your team, and through these councils you have an opportunity to establish and maintain good working relationships.

If you fail to maintain outstanding working relationships as you establish the neighborhood watch, you may be putting your job in jeopardy. I believe it's why we see so much turnover in the CISO ranks. CISOs aren't focused on keeping relationships central to their program. Those of us who get fired usually do so because we've failed to invest in relationships. Hopefully, this book has convinced you of the need to spend more time with others, cultivating good working relationships.

The flip side of effective governance occurs when you get the "invisible middle finger" instead of a hand of partnership from those who resist or resent your involvement in their security decision-making. I've always encountered a handful of teams that play respectfully with you, but silently don't want anything to do with you or your program. They're operating independently from your processes, out of arrogance or self-centeredness. Although they behave politely in meetings and say all the right things, the minute the meeting is over, they have no intention of doing anything that was discussed. They do all they can to stay as far away as possible. You know who they are.

They don't consider themselves neighbors in the neighborhood watch, but operate from a point of independence and self-sufficiency. They may resent you as the security leader or not respect your skills, believing you have little to offer them, so why bother to be involved with you and your team? These folks are not good corporate citizens. Without strong company leadership directing them to "play" with the rest of us, they will be rogues in your environment.

In situations like this, it helps to keep in mind that the security game is played out over many laps around the track. Some teams need more time before playing nicely with the rest of the company. In some situations, I'm not sure you ever really win them over, but your goal should be to get them to a place where they participate in your governance processes and contribute to the overall security of the company, which benefits everyone. Be patient with groups that give you the invisible middle finger. In the absence of good leadership from above, kindness and patience is your best approach in dealing with this crowd.

Understanding the Risks to Giving Your Job Away

As I've highlighted, the transition of security functions to other teams began in the late '90s and early 2000s, and no doubt this trend will continue into the future. As a security leader, you are responsible for a function consisting of a workforce of many neighbors, each playing a part in the neighborhood watch. However, risks come with this type of distributed operating environment. I list a few of those risks in this section, with suggestions on how to navigate your way through them.

RISKY SITUATION 1

In this situation, the team that "owns" a piece of the security pie isn't performing its security responsibilities very well. This is a tough situation to be in. The problem is that company leadership most likely views you as responsible and accountable for security in this area, and changing this perception will be hard. You're at best able to influence the team members, but ultimately they are doing the work. What do you do in a situation like this?

First you need to do a better job educating leadership on the roles and responsibilities of key IT and engineering teams. Although you may never present management with RACI charts, you nonetheless should convey the key messages of those charts to leadership and management. You should emphasize the viewpoint of the neighborhood watch, and the importance of everyone being involved, to help them understand. This situation will pop up again since you don't "own" the security in many areas, but the company leadership believes you should or do.

If you encounter this situation, tell the truth, but do so in a way that is favorable to the system owners. For example, indicate that they're making lots of progress, that they've come a long way over the past year, and that they started with little to no security controls.

Focus on the road map for this area, and where you hope to be in the next six months. I've found that praising the team for their accomplishments, even if they are not where you'd like them to be, will serve you better than telling the blatant truth and throwing them under the bus. This doesn't serve you well.

The next thing you could try to do is meet with the underperforming team to review one of the many industry frameworks that enumerate the security controls possible for the systems they own. Often I've found that merely reviewing the section of the NIST framework relating to their systems helps them see the need for increased security. Using the framework allows you to raise awareness among the team, without the message being delivered from their peers from the InfoSec team. It almost always works. Give it a try.

RISKY SITUATION 2

You may also encounter a team responsible for the security of a function that is making poor security choices. Team members may be buying tools that don't integrate well into the company's security architecture, or may be choosing to run the tool so infrequently that it's rendered ineffective (for example, monthly). How do you handle this situation?

My recommendation here is again to be patient and kind. This team doesn't work for you, so keep in mind that your interactions will be more influence based than directive. Although the system owner may not make the choices you would like, they are taking ownership over their area, and for this they should be acknowledged and praised. As I have said, I like to view progress in terms of laps around the track. In this case, patience with the team will mean that during the next lap, they will have the chance to improve upon their decisions and move security forward. In addition, between now and then, you can bring in security training courses that hopefully move them in the right direction.

Finally, praising the team members in front of their management usually causes them to drop any walls they might have between your two teams. Once they know that you are genuinely seeking their success, you'll find them to be more willing to look to you and your team for input and guidance. This is a win for everyone.

RISKY SITUATION 3

In the third risky situation, you may find yourself working with a team that is difficult to work with. The team members don't want anything to do with your team, and they make that blatantly clear. You've probably never encountered this, right? If not, count your blessings. I see it frequently. As I mentioned earlier, it's the classic invisible middle finger situation, and like surgery, it needs to be handled delicately.

If you haven't personally seen or felt the invisible middle fingers, you may have missed them. Here's what they've looked like from my experience. One of your client teams will meet with you, but once the meeting is over, you know they have zero intention of doing anything that was just discussed. Before you hit the door of the conference room, they're grinning at each other and nodding their heads, acknowledging to each other that the meeting was a colossal waste of time, and that they realize there is little to no consequence for ignoring company security policy or anything that was just discussed. They're just playing you, and you got played.

This leads me to yet another guiding principle: go where you're wanted. There's lots of work for you and your team. There's all the work you're directly responsible for, and there's all the work you must be involved in because you're the head of cybersecurity. So knowing your time is limited, work with those who want to work with you. In time, the outliers will come into the fold. In the meantime, patience is your strong card. Play it often.

Working with Your New Neighbors

As I mentioned previously, Deloitte decomposed the InfoSec space into more than 175 subcomponents. Outside of your team, few could name even 25 of the areas. You'll never be staffed to secure 175 areas, so just accept that you'll need help, and spend your time getting others involved to ensure more areas within InfoSec are covered for the company. Now that you understand that the neighborhood watch is your remit, how do you get it started? How do you get others involved so that they can take responsibility for their systems and areas?

Let's look at the network services team as an example. Your first meeting with this team should be over lunch with the sole purpose of connecting on a personal basis. Do not discuss work. If you have a team, assign one of your folks to this area as a collateral duty—meaning this isn't their full-time job, but rather a secondary duty, working through influence only. It's their job to work with network services to raise awareness of the many security controls available and to be mindful of security in all they do. Much of today's networking functions are really security tasks.

I believe that at most companies, network security has been relinquished to the network services team. Needless to say, this team is a big partner of yours. These team members are so important that I recommend you offer them network security courses. This will ensure they are educated on the security of the systems under their ownership. This will cost a little bit of money, but once again the ROI is off the charts.

At the second meeting with network services, I recommend you begin the discussion of roles and responsibilities for the security of the network. You could start with your charter, with statements like this:

> *IT management and staff, working with their business counterparts and InfoSec, are accountable for the security of the data and systems that support their business processes and goals. They are responsible for implementing and maintaining systems, in accordance with InfoSec policy and standards.*

Usually, other teams want to "own" the entire space of their services and don't want others, like the InfoSec team, involved in their work. Working within a model of shared responsibilities is a delicate balance, and it requires management finesse to pull off. In these partnership situations, you need their cooperation, so allow them to embrace security at their own pace. I've found that over time, the other teams are actually doing more for security than I had hoped for. It's a beautiful situation.

Helpful Hints for Working with Other Teams

Take every opportunity to recognize the many teams and individuals who move the company toward increased security. Public recognition of others always pays dividends, often in ways you can't fully appreciate. It also has the effect of showing others that you put them first and are willing to acknowledge their contributions in front of others. This is contagious. Make recognition of others a part of every presentation. Be known as a leader who gives credit to others.

Next, meet with all the other teams performing security work at least quarterly. If, for example, they are securing end points (like the client engineering team), I suggest monthly or every other month. This team is so important and central to your strategy that it warrants meeting with them more frequently. I recommend that all the meetings be over lunch. I try to open every meeting with 15 minutes of personal connection and not discuss business or the meeting objectives. This can wait.

Next, maybe twice a year, meet with the management of every team with responsibilities for security. Take the time during these meetings to acknowledge all their contributions and how appreciative you are of their accomplishments. Let the boss hear from you about the great work they've accomplished and the improvements in security in their area. You want a professional partner for life? Praise them in front of their boss and you've sealed the deal.

Finally, make plans to offer professional security training courses to these other teams. All techies love professional training, and offering cybersecurity technical training classes shows that you care. Before the classes are offered, meet with the instructor to discuss the course objectives and ensure that their materials align with your environment and policy. If done correctly, these courses can be your extended voice to the other teams. This should be a huge win for you, so plan it wisely.

Conclusion

As I said at the start of this chapter and elsewhere in this book, your only hope for securing the company's information assets is to get everyone involved. In particular, you need the IT and engineering teams involved, as they own most of the company's systems. Since the early 2000s, the trend has been to shift security responsibilities to the system owners. Many in the company, especially the leadership, may view the CISO as responsible and accountable for InfoSec, but in actuality the CISO is usually able to only influence other teams and nudge them toward greater security. Operating in this type of environment takes more time to get security right across the company.

As you work with your new "neighbors" and give your job away, focus on what matters most. Be patient with your new neighbors. View the journey with them as having many laps around the track. Praise them as often as possible, especially to their management.

Finally, treat everyone with kindness. Ignore the invisible middle fingers. Go where you're wanted and work with those willing to work with you. Bring in professional training courses to enhance the skill sets of other teams. And remember, governance grows in importance as you add new neighbors into the neighborhood watch. If you practice just some of these actions, you'll be well on your way to building a solid InfoSec program.

9

Step 6: Organize Your InfoSec Team

The preceding chapter discussed the importance of partnering with others in the company to share InfoSec responsibilities. I urged you to give parts of your job away and to place the responsibility for security on the system owners. Why does this make sense? Two reasons. The first is to enable the concept of the neighborhood watch, with the goal of getting everyone in the company to do their part. The second is that your InfoSec department is likely grossly under-resourced for the task at hand.

From my experience, all InfoSec departments have one thing in common: not enough staff or money to protect the company's information assets from the litany of threats they face. Like the many heads of the mythical hydra, threats to security seem to multiply with each new technology. So few companies have the staff or budget to keep up with those threats and demands for InfoSec services.

We make choices about which "crisis" to handle among the many crises that pop up every day. It's an exercise in risk management triage every day, all day. I don't know about you, but I've always been under-resourced and never had the luxury of downtime or quiet time. It's 911 all day. It's the nature of our work. As I've said before, InfoSec is like a game of hockey: fast and full contact, with no bench time. It's not a job or career for sprinters. Our jobs are marathons with no opportunities to stop or catch your breath.

So how do you hope to survive in this situation? The answer is the neighborhood watch. It's your only hope. Get everyone involved, especially other technical teams. It's time to imagine a world where the security knowledge required to protect the "town" is in the hands of the company's staff. If you subscribe to the neighborhood watch model, I believe you can be very effective as a security leader with a small staff.

Identifying the Type of Talent You'll Need

If you're new to your job, you're in one of two situations: you've either just inherited an existing InfoSec team, or you have to build one. Both have their challenges. My preference is to be able to hire your own people and build the team you need. Let me start with that scenario.

In my seven-step process, you need a certain type of security person in order to be successful: technical types with good interpersonal skills. This type of staff member will make life easy for you and will enable you to build the InfoSec program the company wants. Not having staff with technical *and* interpersonal skills will make your work much harder and inevitably lead you into difficult management situations.

I recommend that everyone on your team be college graduates, preferably with engineering degrees. This ensures they have the theory of computer science/engineering and understand the computing stack. College grads are usually more agile and can easily grasp the technical nuances of new areas. This sort of agility provides you with the flexibility you'll need as you reassign people to different areas, as one team member backfills for another.

Next they should have expertise in some area of computing. It doesn't matter which area of technology, but they must be deep in that area. If you have people with college degrees from the right disciplines and they've spent time in at least one area of IT and acquired expertise in that area, then they have a good foundation to be successful as an InfoSec type.

Finally, and probably the most difficult attribute to find among the technical people I just described, but that is essential to the success of your program, are interpersonal skills—or people skills. Unless you have a large InfoSec team, you should not sacrifice on this point. It's better to have someone with fewer technical skills and abilities than to compromise on this area. Let me say it again: your new hire must have great people skills, no exceptions. I've worked with and retained technically brilliant people who had zero to no people skills. They were often toxic to the organization and found themselves in technical battles and disagreements with their colleagues whenever they had the opportunity. These types have the natural ability to piss people off without even knowing it. And it happens far too often. I now avoid these types. They're too expensive to maintain.

As a reminder, relationships are the *foundation* upon which you will build your program, and at the heart of relationships are people skills. If your team members don't have people skills, their value to your team greatly drops. It will be your team members who evangelize the security messages throughout the company. Great people skills will allow them to manage through the sticky situations that often arise for security types—for example, the handling of an incident or the discovery that one of the system administrators has been grossly negligent in their responsibilities. If you take away only one message from this chapter, let it be this: you need folks with great interpersonal skills. Without them, building an InfoSec program will be a continual uphill battle.

Managing a Preexisting Team

If you're inheriting a preexisting team, you potentially have your hands full. This is much more difficult than hiring your own team. Some of the people you inherit will have wanted your job, or at least thought they should be considered for your job. Others on the team will have close relationships with your predecessor and are likely still in contact with that person. Still others will question your qualifications and be tapping into their network of people in the industry to get the skinny on you. In the end, this team isn't "yours," and you'll face a potential landmine of possibilities when you take over a preexisting team.

So how do you evaluate your newly adopted team members? Here's what I've learned from being in that situation a time or two. I suggest you meet with each member of your team as soon as possible. You're not going to make any decisions based on these initial conversations, but they are the beginning of your evaluations of them. I would also ask them what their core technical competencies are, and what they've been doing within the company during their tenure. From this first meeting, you're evaluating two competencies: technical skills and interpersonal skills.

People skills are the easiest to identify, and you can usually tell during these meetings who the keepers are. To some extent, you're looking for salespeople, individuals who can work with others while not pissing them off. You want people who can run meetings, make presentations in front of various groups, and walk the halls and evangelize the organization with you. Security types who can do these things are worth their weight in gold. They can do more to advance a security program than anyone else on the team. Those who can't do this may have much to offer, but they may be limited to the technical side only.

Once you've met all the team members, I usually plan for a meeting of all staff members, where I can begin to share the direction I'd like to take the team as well as my expectations. This staff meeting is important, and you need to be well prepared. Understand and practice each of your talking points and what you hope your team takes away from the meeting.

Note

Over the years, I've refined a set of bedrock expectations for the smooth functioning of any team. I keep this list in a journal so I have it ready whenever I need it. I typically review it a couple of times a year, even when I've been with a company for four or five years. Team members need to hear these talking points over and over, and the list also helps new team members who may not have been part of the team from the onset. Going over the list in staff meetings a couple of times a year allows me to reinforce our direction and the expectations we have as a team.

At this initial staff meeting, share your philosophy or approach to InfoSec. Let them know why you were hired and your beliefs on how best to protect the company's information assets. Hopefully, this will all be about the neighborhood watch.

Once your vision and approach are shared, tell everyone they have x number of days to decide whether they'd like to be part of your team. You're basically asking them to decide if they are in or out. They can use this time to decide whether they want to be part of something new or would prefer to take their talents elsewhere. I usually give them 30 days. The difficulty is in identifying those who give you lip service that "they're in," and who show some demonstration of a willingness to stay, but really aren't in at all. My message is simple: if I don't see a clear and compelling demonstration, it's time to part ways.

Your biggest impediment to growing the program won't be the resistance you receive on the streets; it will be the resistance from the naysayers on your team who have not bought into the new direction. It's better to have a team of 3 who are all "rowing" in the same direction than to have 10 guys with a couple of naysayers quietly working against you.

Good luck in your early tenure, as the message you convey to your team as well as the expectations you have of them are important for them to hear. I also have a document of guiding principles developed over the past 20 years that I share with everyone during these first few meetings. The principles cover such topics as the importance of operating with humility and kindness toward others, treating others as we'd like to be treated, listening first, and seeking to understand before we speak.

Where You Report in the Organization Matters

I started this book by making the argument that nobody understands InfoSec and nobody really cares about it. To support my argument, look at where you report in your organizational chart. A recent Ponemon Institute study (*https://*

oreil.ly/vAunm) reported on the CIO & Leader website indicates that about 50% of us report to the CIO.

But placing InfoSec under the CIO creates so many conflicts of interest. For example, the results of pentests or vulnerability assessments can be overlooked because the system owners are busy with other "more important" business priorities. Or system owners may resist sending logs to the central logging service because they say they are too busy with other higher priorities, when in fact they just don't want to provide others with visibility into their administrative activities or negligence. Reporting to the CIO also often means that security initiatives will take a back seat to IT projects, which compete for system owner time.

If you report to the CIO, the likelihood of being moved to somewhere else in the organization is next to zero. CIOs like to have the InfoSec team under their wings, to control our work and the message communicated throughout the company. It also looks good on their resumes. Your team also puts lots of points on the board for them, which they desperately need in our new world of growing importance for InfoSec. You also probably present to the board a couple times a year, and they do not, but they can take credit for your presentation and come along with you while you do. Finally, and where it hits home the hardest, is that smart CIOs don't want the scrutiny that would come from an InfoSec department reporting on the shortcomings of the IT department. This would happen if you reported to someone else in the organizational chart. So if you report to the CIO, learn how to live with it, because it's not going to change anytime soon.

Working with the Infrastructure Team

Once you've identified the keepers on your team, it's time to distribute the work of InfoSec to those who've elected to stay. It should come as no surprise that the majority of the work in InfoSec is focused on the infrastructure team. The infrastructure comprises all those components upon which the company's business data resides: cloud service providers, virtual machines, Amazon Machine Images (AMIs), EC2 instances, networks, operating systems, end points, servers, the data center, and so forth.

I like to assign each security team member to one of those areas as their primary customer. These team members are responsible for attending their customers' staff meetings, for working with them to secure the components under their control, for building baselines, developing security processes, configuring systems, researching security issues, and staying side by side with their customer team members while they improve the security of their own systems and data.

When issues arise in these areas, it is your team member's responsibility to work with the customer to solve them. It's a model that works well and allows for individuals on the team to work initially in areas of their own choosing. These assignments will represent about 50% of their job. If you have only 5 folks on your team but 10 infrastructure areas, combine the areas logically and assign each team member to 2 areas. These areas will be their customers, their client base. In addition to these infrastructure areas, they'll be given application support areas and other business unit responsibilities, depending on how your company is organized.

This is where the need for people skills is really required. Those who are successful will literally blitz their areas with their presence, emails, and presentations. In a relatively short time, the InfoSec message will get through to their colleagues, and the partnership for securing company assets will have begun.

Organizing your team is one of the four cornerstones of your program, as I outlined in Chapter 6. You can't afford to get this wrong or hire weak players. Alignment with the organization matters, so each InfoSec team member will likely have multiple client groups. If you've selected the members well, your team will be an agile group with the ability to serve multiple clients at the same time.

The really good ones flourish in this environment and operate as if they're running their own business. Once they get the philosophy of risk advisory, they can skillfully move from one department of the company to the next. Getting your people assigned and positioned into the business units is key and will net huge returns quickly.

Dealing with Toxic Security Leaders

In many of my security leadership positions, I was often hired on the heels of an InfoSec leader whose approach to InfoSec was absolute. They were security purists: security types who believe security is an all-or-nothing game. They live in a binary world of step functions; you're either secure or you're not.

They believe security is attainable if it achieves their idea of security. They lack business sense and misunderstand the concept of risk management. They take their job personally and seldom compromise. To compromise is to sell out or admit defeat. They are often aliens in the companies where they work—strangers, unable to get comfortable in the environment or ever settle in. These security leaders blame the organization for "not getting it." The resistance they encounter is often rationalized as "the company doesn't get it." They believe that if the company understood security, it would embrace them and their approach.

These types often lack the self-awareness to understand that the organization forms antibodies against them in an effort to rid them of the toxicity they bring. The host is defending itself against them.

The concept of alignment is foreign to the absolute security type. They see their lot in life as one of martyrdom and view the persecutions as a badge of honor. They're misguided and out of touch. They wish the organization understood the value of security, but it never does, and they therefore exist like foreigners from a strange land. Separation from the company is inevitable.

Eventually, the antibodies get so great they are removed completely. The organization excels without them, and there's a sigh of relief among all when they depart. I could write a book about these types and the harm they cause their companies. Let's save that for another day.

I have often been hired into this type of environment and faced the challenge of cleaning up the mess they left behind. Relationships must be mended. Credibility must be established, and a whole new complexion put on the face of InfoSec. Following one of these Genghis Khan–type leaders isn't easy. It is, however, how I learned the value of relationships and developed the neighborhood watch model. If you do follow someone who left the InfoSec team in shambles, you've inherited the challenge of turning things around.

Turning Around an InfoSec Enemy

Most of you will encounter some passive-aggressive behaviors from other teams within the company. I've encountered this everywhere I've worked, especially during the early days on the job. At one company, it was the network services team members. They gave me no love. Their history with the InfoSec team was bad to the bone.

When I met the leader of the network services team, I was taken aback by their suspicion of me and their sarcastic tone. They'd seen many of my predecessors come and go. Each was equally toxic and harmful to the organization as the next. All were "flamers," crash-and-burn types, and this leader didn't like any of them. They assumed I was cut from the same cloth, and I couldn't blame them.

After meeting with the network services leader, I assigned a new security engineer to work with their team. My team member did not know the history between the departments, and, like me, they were fresh meat for the old-timers in network services. In many ways, I felt as if I were feeding my team member to the lions.

I accompanied them to our first staff meeting and introduced them to the 15 members of the network services team. I took a few minutes to share with them our new approach to InfoSec, and how we wanted to establish the neighborhood watch with them. I asked for their patience and their feedback if we got off track in any way. You could have heard a pin drop. Not one of them said a word. All of them had a look of disbelief on their faces, and I wasn't sure whether that was good or bad. I trotted on. I shared with them that my team member would be the InfoSec representative to their team, and all matters relating to InfoSec should include them. I went so far as to suggest a cubicle in their area be given to my team member as a place to sit when they were there.

After a moment, people started asking questions. We responded to them all. We both understood the challenge ahead of us. This was a rough group. They had strong bonds among themselves and had built up antibodies to all interactions relating to the InfoSec team.

We listened to their stories about the atrocities committed during previous InfoSec regimes and how they were still paying for them. I listened to the systems they were required to deploy in response to audits that were driven up their backsides by my predecessors. I listened to the verbal lashings they'd received from the CIO about their carelessness for security. Their resistance to security unified them. I had been in this position before; it was not new to me. We had to approach them with an extended hand and a willingness to support their efforts. But I realized the odds were stacked against us.

The engineer assigned to them from my team was technical and possessed good interpersonal skills. They were one of a rare breed whom I've worked with over the years. They loved both the widgets and the people. They were a perfect fit. They also had thick skin and welcomed the challenge. Even as a new hire like myself, they volunteered for the job, knowing the group was a pack of wolves.

I coached my team member about our approach, as they wanted to be successful. They were moldable. They jumped straight into network services with both feet. They immersed themselves in the network services staff meetings, made presentations, and worked shoulder to shoulder with their engineers. They learned the network architecture, reviewed the firewall rule sets, and spent time on designs and system configurations. They assisted in the provisioning process and helped with audit remediation. Whatever the network services team was doing, they were there. They became a part of the team. Their presence alone had an immediate impact for good. They spent lots of time with them, and actually was given a cubicle in their spaces. They were a natural, and it was easy for them to partner and be accepted. The plan worked brilliantly.

While they were immersed in all their work, we also spun up several network security courses for the network services team—courses like network pentesting, securing firewalls and DMZs, and network security monitoring. Many network services team members attended the courses. The word spread among their team that the courses were high speed and worth their time. Within just a few months, we had converts. The network services team appreciated the training. No one had brought world-class training in-house before. The courses were a huge win for us all.

Within a short time, the network services team members bonded to us. They became our partners. They took ownership over the security of their systems. We were no longer viewed as enemies of their team, and the animosity between the teams was gone. When trade-offs between security and performance were raised, we rolled in their favor. In the early days, we didn't insist on security but let them make the decisions. After a couple of years, several of the network services team members went so far as to ask how they could get on the security team. We were honored.

Defining Roles and Responsibilities of Team Members

Now that each of your team members has been assigned to the various departments, it's time to define what they will do with their new customers. I suggest your team members initiate their new relationships over hosted lunches. I even budget for lunches in the InfoSec annual budget. It's one of the smallest line items in the budget, but the best spent money of all my expenses.

For the first lunch, I suggest that business not be discussed. Keep it all on a personal level. I've found that asking everyone to introduce themselves and share their favorite Netflix series is usually a great place to start. People love to share their favorite series, and this will easily take up most of the time. If you run out of time, ask for their favorite movies.

At the second hosted lunch, it would be a good time to introduce an industry standard framework that touches on the IT or engineering function they are assigned to. For example, if they are assigned to an end-user computing group, I like to share the NIST 800 and flip to the section on securing end points. The goal of this meeting is strictly education, to get the client team to start thinking about security and what they've implemented on the systems they administer.

No doubt, a look at industry frameworks will lead to a discussion from the team about which controls they should target for the next version of the system they are rolling out. Leave this up to them. You're just a consultant at this point, and the decision is theirs. It is like magic to watch, though: all you did was present an industry framework of best practices, and in two simple hosted lunches, you've got them making a road map of changes they'd like to make.

During future meetings, you can begin to discuss which controls make sense in your environment. This will lead to a gap in controls and a discussion of whether any of the missing controls should be implemented. You'll be amazed at how powerful it is to merely project an industry framework and see how the discussion goes. Other frameworks that make sense (depending on the team you're meeting with) are OWASP, CIS Top 20, CSA, and ISO standards.

Next, I suggest your team member assigned to each area present a defense-in-depth model, as shown in Chapter 6, Figure 6-1. A good place to start is to ask them to identify all the security controls (logical, physical, and administrative) they've implemented for their system. Documenting this on the concentric circle they own will be a powerful visual. At future meetings, have your team member share the InfoSec charter, policy, and SIRP that you developed in step 2 (in Chapter 5). Finally, have your team member identify one technical training course to offer to this team.

Remember, security is a shared responsibility among all staff members and the InfoSec team. The team must be organized to serve the various business units of the company. Each team member should be assigned to an infrastructure team, and/or one of the application services or business unit teams.

Structuring Your Team

To help you get a feel for how to structure your team, here is a sample of the responsibilities for one of my team members and their goals:

InfoSec road map and architecture

1. Develop/update a defense-in-depth architecture to reflect all the security controls within your assigned area. Present it to management for review and feedback.

Improve customer relationships

1. Identify team-building activities for IT groups that struggle with InfoSec policy.
2. Make four staff presentations to the various IT groups.
3. Ensure positive working relationships with all customers, third-party vendors, and contractors.

Educate and raise awareness among staff

1. Conduct 12 lunch-and-learns.
2. Collaborate with our communications person to promote awareness. Share with the team the items you're working on and solicit feedback.
3. Collaborate with other InfoSec members to prepare a presentation for all IT areas. Make quarterly staff presentations to the various IT groups you support.

Build an extended InfoSec team that includes representatives from each IT area

1. Conduct monthly lunch meetings with agendas. Have the agendas reviewed by the head of InfoSec and presented at an InfoSec staff meeting.
2. Advertise the InfoSec meetings and ensure that representatives from the areas you support participate.
3. Chair the meeting as required.
4. Develop a list of the top 10 risks. Present this list to the CIO.
5. Validate all security policies and standards with the team.
6. Provide feedback to members' sponsors on their involvement.

7. Own the action items from the meetings and follow up with the assigned areas.

Manage the top 10 risks across IT

1. Manage the top 10 risks in assigned areas. Track progress against all high-risk categories.
2. Develop metrics to track progress against all high-risk categories.

InfoSec representative to network services

1. Attend network services staff meetings.
2. Ensure participation in all projects and provide updates at the InfoSec staff meeting.
3. Ensure that network assets are scanned for vulnerabilities and patched per policies.
4. Participate in all audits that impact network services.
5. Be responsible for all security matters as they relate to network services.
6. Conduct pentest(s) and provide results back to network services management.

InfoSec representative to sales and marketing IT

1. Be responsible for all security matters as they relate to sales and marketing IT.
2. Conduct training for sales and marketing IT staff.
3. Attend staff meetings.
4. Participate in all projects.

IDS project

1. Complete the IDS project.
2. Ensure that all IDSs are operational and providing feeds to our monitoring service.
3. Obtain IDS certification for all installed systems.

4. Provide updates to InfoSec staff on the status of the project.

5. Manage all contracted support personnel.

Pentest

1. Lead and manage one announced pentest. Ensure that all areas (external web and cloud services, network perimeter, telco, wireless, and social engineering) are assessed and measured.

2. Track metrics for each assessment.

3. Develop a spreadsheet or reporting mechanism to store findings and remediation efforts.

4. Collaborate with IT groups to remediate findings.

5. Identify staff members who have moved the security boulder up the hill and recognize them in front of their peers and possibly monetarily.

6. Share all reports and progress at weekly staff meetings.

Audits (team goal)

1. Support corporate audits as required.

2. Support IT business unit audits.

Contract management (team goal)

1. Perform contract management duties as they relate to your assigned areas.

Perform on-call duties

1. Respond to managed security service provider (MSSP) alerts.

2. Manage InfoSec alerts received.

3. Manage the SIRP.

4. Respond to all emails received.

Common goals
Comply with all standards, policies, processes, and tools.

These are a lot of goals for one individual to carry, but I remind the team they are aspirational. We review everyone's goals regularly at staff meetings so as to make adjustments along the way. No one feels overwhelmed or pressured by their goals.

As you can see by reviewing the goals, each team member is assigned to several business units within and outside the IT and engineering departments. Depending on the staff member and their level of experience, they may also have responsibilities to support one of the big-five departments: legal, HR, corporate security, corporate audit, and members of the C-level suites. In general, these groups are so important that I seldom delegate this responsibility but do most of the liaison myself.

Conclusion

Most InfoSec teams have one thing in common: they are grossly under-resourced to protect the company. You will never have enough staff or money to get the job done. This is our reality. I've seen only one or two exceptions in the financial services industry and among Silicon Valley tech companies.

For this reason, hiring the right type of engineers with outstanding people skills allows you to assign them to multiple teams. The process laid out in this book emphasizes relationships and team building, so people skills are nonnegotiable for success. Don't hire someone who will create more trouble than they're worth. You don't have the time to manage them. Instead, hire energetic engineers who love to work with people and you'll set yourself up for success over the long run. I've followed this rule for over 20 years, and it has never let me down. It has ensured my success and allowed me to build the InfoSec function the company wants from my team.

Step 7: Measure What Matters

In Chapter 9, I discussed the importance of having team members who possessed both technical and interpersonal skills. I made this claim because those on your team who are able to walk the halls of your organization spreading the good news of InfoSec while also participating in technical meetings are the individuals on your team who really move your program forward. Once you have your people in place, this next step is about measuring your progress toward a particular goal or objective. This chapter covers the value of metrics, which ones to focus on, and how to use them to improve security for the company.

Why Measure?

If you choose to build your InfoSec program following the seven steps I've laid out, measuring your program's progress along the way will greatly help your cause. Measurement is the tool used to convince management of the progress you're making year after year.

You'll use your metrics to highlight to management that their investment in InfoSec is paying off. The front office speaks the language of money. Therefore, you should show in numbers the ROI from InfoSec.

One of the best ways I've discovered to show this ROI is to illustrate that the company is more secure this year than last year. The way to do that is by capturing a couple of key metrics. Without the hard data, leadership is just taking your word for it.

The tough part will be convincing them you're measuring the right items and that these items reflect a mature, self-defending organization. This is your job. The use of metrics shows leadership that the InfoSec program is moving in the right direction (and that you were a wise choice to lead the team).

Understanding What to Measure

So now the question is, what to measure? You have a lot of metrics to choose from. but which ones matter to leadership, especially early in your tenure? If you've ever visited Securitymetrics.org (*http://www.securitymetrics.org/*), you've seen the hundreds of security metrics available. They're all good metrics. But which ones *really* matter?

Before deciding what to measure, let's identify the objective we want to achieve, and then determine how best to measure our progress toward that objective. Based on the previous six steps, our objective is to influence the culture toward individual responsibility for security over the information assets under their control in an effort to establish the neighborhood watch. So which metrics matter when you're building a self-defending organization? Which metrics capture staff's ability to partner with you and perform their role to defend the company's information assets? Those are the objectives we want to measure progress toward.

To measure progress in creating a self-defending organization, two metrics surface. They are closely related to each other. I've used these 2 metrics for the better part of the last 20 years, and they resonate well with company leadership because they are simple:

- Metric 1: Can staff recognize a policy violation when it occurs, and do they know how to report it?

- Metric 2: Can staff identify a phishing email, and do they know how to report it?

These two metrics reflect the overall awareness level among staff members, and their ability to report policy violations or suspected security incidents when they happen. Tracking these metrics will indicate your progress toward protecting the company's information assets and establishing the neighborhood watch. If you train staff on the information security policy that applies to their areas, and measure their ability to respond, then you're moving toward your objective of influencing the culture toward security. That's it. These metrics are simple, make sense, and resonate with company management.

These two metrics may seem like the same metric, but they're not. The first one requires the recognition by staff of policy violations as they occur in their area of responsibility. For example, a system administrator might recognize that a system is not protected by two-factor authentication, and either reach out to the

InfoSec team for help or integrate the system into the company's two-factor tools and processes. This recognition of policy violations requires that they have knowledge of the applicable policies that apply to their responsibilities for InfoSec.

The second metric applies to *all* staff and is specifically focused on the staff's ability to recognize and report fraudulent emails. This metric measures the degree of skepticism held by staff as they process company email.

Both metrics require staff training. Metric 1 requires information security policy training relating to their specific area of responsibilities. Metric 2 requires training that enables staff to analyze and identify fraudulent emails that make it to their inboxes. The goal of a phishing program is to raise the level of skepticism held by staff as they approach their email.

The remainder of this chapter focuses on the simple implementation of these two metrics. I provide specific ways you can capture these numbers, the fun you can have with them, and the benefit they provide to other areas of InfoSec policy. I believe that once you see the wisdom in their use, you'll join me in using them exclusively with company leadership. As I said, I've used them for 20 years, with very positive feedback.

Recognizing Policy Violations

Most staff at your company make one broad assumption about InfoSec: they wrongly believe somebody else is doing it for them. Most staff believe it's somebody else's job to protect systems, data, and intellectual property. They assume you and your team are "stirring the sauce" to keep things secure. You know this isn't true, and you must correct this misassumption.

Outside of IT or engineering departments, nobody spends much or any time on system and data security. Again, they assume someone else is doing it for them. They assume security is built into the systems they use. That the network firewalls protect the company. That laptops are secured by tools provided by the IT department. Without education, staff operate with a sense of carelessness toward InfoSec, because they believe security is baked into the systems or processes. They conclude that everything is OK, because somebody else has taken care of it. Most staff members are focused on getting their jobs done, and they assume IT is protecting their systems and data.

To influence the culture, you have to address this assumption and the resulting consequence—namely, that employees don't view InfoSec as *their* responsibility. Making InfoSec everyone's responsibility is the focus and goal of your security awareness and education program; your awareness program will go hand in hand with your metrics program. The two are inseparable.

As staff become more educated on their roles and responsibilities, you influence the culture toward greater degrees of security, and move the organization in the direction of self-defense. But as you educate staff, you have to measure the improvements in staff awareness as they apply to their responsibilities. Employees need routine checks or report cards to see whether they understand their responsibilities for InfoSec. When you start the awareness program, you'll want to catch the baseline of knowledge among the staff. This will be your starting point.

To move the organization toward the neighborhood watch, you need everyone doing their part, and this means being able to identify and report security policy violations when they happen. My test to understand the staff's ability to detect policy violations and report them aims to answer this question: is a staff member at the farthest office from headquarters able to identify and report on simple security policy violations when they happen? If they can, you've done your job and achieved your objective.

Why do I target the farthest office from headquarters? I assume the staff at headquarters will get a disproportionate amount of awareness training because that location usually has the biggest component of the InfoSec team. Therefore, testing those farthest from headquarters will give you a good sense as to the effectiveness of your education and awareness program.

The Mother of All Metrics: Phishing Tests

Phishing should have a special place in the life of all InfoSec organizations. For more than 15 years, we as an industry haven't made much progress in the area of phishing. The numbers as reported by Symantec's Internet Security Threat Report (*https://oreil.ly/8vk82*) from 2019 showed that phishing was the initial entry point for over 90% of all company breaches. This statistic dropped in only the last five years or so. Since 2015, phishing stats have fallen into the mid-80th percentile, which still makes phishing the most attractive tool for hackers. Conducting phishing tests and phishing training exercises among staff is a valuable exercise.

The few companies I've found that do have phishing programs do it to check a box. This is unfortunate. The phishing program, if done properly, offers many benefits to the InfoSec program and to protecting information assets throughout the company. If the industry metrics are true that nearly 85% of all breaches are traced back to a phishing email,[1] understanding your staff's ability to recognize and report a phishing email is a metric well worth your time.

Considering this fact, I suggest you make phishing exercises a top priority. If rogue organizations phish your organization every day, why wouldn't you prioritize this as well? We can see from the data that having a phishing program is important to an overall InfoSec program. But if this is true, why don't more security programs focus on it? I believe it's because this work isn't sexy to most InfoSec types. Second, it requires the hard work of end-user training. It's easier to implement a tool instead. However, I believe that your staff's ability to defend against phishing emails is the key metric to monitor.

Each year, I faithfully read the internet threat reports published by Symantec, Mandiant, Verizon, and Cisco to understand the numbers of our industry, phishing being one of them. The industry isn't making great progress in this area because identifying a phish remains primarily a human endeavor. It requires the recipient of the email to make a judgment call regarding the authenticity of that email. No tool on the market does this yet. And teaching staff how to detect fraudulent emails isn't exciting work that most CISOs want to do. I've not heard CISOs at conferences standing around bragging about their phishing programs. But mention the latest cool tool from XYZ Company, and they all have it!

As a result of its importance, a phishing metric is always a part of my presentations to the board of directors. When I explain why I capture the phishing metric, every member of senior management and the board gets it. It makes sense. They also get the concept of the neighborhood watch and how phishing relates to that goal. I further explain that the true goal of any phishing program is to *raise the level of skepticism* among staff when they approach their email. If staff members look with skepticism at each email they open, and they know how to identify the markers of a phishing email, then you've achieved your goal.

I use the company's phishing program along with some key pentests and red team exercises to drive and assess the company's overall maturity in InfoSec. My goal is to phish the entire company every day, and to achieve a company-wide failure rate of less than 3%. I track every staff member's scores, and focus additional training on what I like to call the "repeat unrepentant felons" who click everything that comes to their inbox. Your company has them too. For whatever reason, they click all emails, then open everything. Once you identify this short

---

1 See "Verizon Says Phishing Still Drives 90% of Cybersecurity Breaches" (*https://oreil.ly/tlLrL*) at the Graphus Blog.

list of staff members, you can offer them more training or place additional security tools on their laptops to compensate for their tendencies.

The details of how to run a phishing program are outside the scope of this book, but you can do many creative things with the program that provide many benefits to the company, the staff, and its general contribution to the overall security posture of the company. Needless to say, the money I devote to our phishing program is some of the best money I spend.

Social Engineering and Staff Training

Back in the early 2000s when Kevin Mitnick (*https://oreil.ly/43bEb*) was enjoying some notoriety, I hired an outside firm to run an anonymous social engineering assessment. I asked this firm to call 500 employees posing as an IT support person attempting to solve a network problem that required their password to fix. The results were not good. When staff were asked, by an unknown caller, to provide their user ID and password, nearly one in two gave up that information without hesitation; 46% of our employees gave their login ID and password to a stranger on the phone! Yikes. With two phone calls, any intruder could have access to our corporate network.

What did I do? I started a security awareness campaign. It was a blitz, really. It was like dropping leaflets from helicopters across the company. We handed out mouse pads and pens with little security reminders on them. We set up a table at every company event to hand out security swag. We held classes to teach employees about securing their home PCs. The lobby of every building had bowls of fortune cookies, with cute security messages instead of fortunes inside them. We made presentations at every all-staff meeting that would have us. We developed online courses that were entertaining and lasted for less than five minutes. We held lunch-and-learns and provided tips on how to buy a home computer. You name it, we were doing it, and it really paid off.

I hit security awareness hard for a few years, and at the end of each year we brought that same consulting firm back to dial a new set of 500 users. Each year, the numbers dropped dramatically. The responses from staff members were also noted. After the second year of our awareness program, we had staff members asking the *caller* for their names and phone numbers! We also had staff members telling the callers it was against policy to share their password with anyone! Some staff were even noted to slam down the phone on the testers.

After three years, only 4% of the employees gave up any type of sensitive information to unknown callers. Throughout this time, the number of calls to our InfoSec hotline skyrocketed. I had so many people reporting security policy violations to the InfoSec team that I couldn't keep up with the calls. Dropping from a 46% failure rate to a 4% rate in 2 years was amazing. The money I spent on education and training was peanuts compared to what I was spending on security technologies. The difference was staggering.

A quick word of warning, however. When you blitz an entire company with security awareness training and information, you *may* take an employee culture known for being helpful and turn it into a group of very suspicious people. Employees will ask questions and be less trusting of requests for information, even when the requests come from within the company.

I was provided this feedback, that as a result of our awareness initiatives, employees had become ultra-vigilant about *not* sharing information with others over the phone, even when the call originated from internal extensions. The fear was staff were not as friendly as before, and much more suspicious of the authenticity of callers; I believe it's a worthwhile trade-off given the alternatives.

Technology Versus Training

I've introduced you to the key metric I track to reflect progress toward establishing a self-defending company: staff members' ability to identify security policy violations when they occur, and their understanding of how to report them. This metric reflects your progress toward achieving the neighborhood watch.

The key question is, do your employees know those parts of the information security policy that apply to them, and how to report policy violations when those parts are violated? If the answer is yes, you've done your job as a security manager and leader. If the answer is no, you have more work to do in training staff on InfoSec policy as it relates to their job responsibilities. Therefore, simple training of staff on the parts of InfoSec policy that apply to them is key. This will take time for you to understand, but it's worth the effort.

Once you know the InfoSec policy that applies to the various teams, you must craft a training program to teach those responsibilities. I've found the use of humorous video training to be the best tool.

Considering how much companies are willing to spend to keep external adversaries away from their crown jewels, why is there so much resistance to spending a small fraction of that money educating the people who have direct access to those jewels? Think of all the technology you and others within the IT department have implemented to protect the company. All technology is rendered useless if one employee isn't aware of their responsibilities to InfoSec in their day-to-day routine. I can't think of a security control implemented that couldn't be bypassed in some way through the ignorance of staff members.

Conclusion

My claim is simple: devoting time and resources to educating staff on these two metrics is a great use of your time. Nothing will protect your company's information assets like a well-educated employee. Not only is awareness cheap, but the ROI is staggering. No other InfoSec expenditure pays back like a few dollars spent on awareness does.

I believe the job of every InfoSec group is to influence the company culture toward greater degrees of security, as the company allows you to do so. If you can begin to measure and pursue the simple metrics laid out in this chapter, you and your organization can make a significant leap in reducing the attack surface of your environment, without buying a single piece of hardware or software. A well-trained staff member is your best defense, with the neighborhood watch as your goal.

11

Working with the Audit Team

In Chapter 10, I discussed the value of security metrics and which metrics really matter when building your program. Metrics are a valuable tool to convince company management that your efforts are paying off and that the company is getting an ROI from the resources committed to security. The subject of this chapter is working with the audit department.

Your goal in working with this group is to obtain some value from the time spent (or drained) by the audit process. If left unguided, the audit team will spend lots of time on audit endeavors that do not improve the company's InfoSec posture. Few auditors know much about InfoSec. It's your job to partner with the audit department and ensure its efforts move the security needle forward.

The Audit Team Needs Your Help to Be Effective in Cybersecurity

Let me start by saying I'm not a fan of the audit department. Why? Because auditors have taught me over the past 20 years that they don't know how to audit the InfoSec space and rely on external auditors too much for guidance. As a result, much of my time and the InfoSec team's time with auditors is spent on frivolous and insignificant activities. Without close partnership with the InfoSec team, corporate audit activities are often misguided and ineffective at moving the security needle for the good of the company.

As I mentioned in Chapter 4, relationships are the key to your success, and it's nowhere truer than with the audit department. At publicly traded companies, the audit department is a powerful team, often reporting to the board of directors or a chief administration officer of some sort. In my experience, auditors will not reach out to collaborate with you, so it will be up to you to partner with them. If you're able to form a good working relationship with the chief auditor, you're on the road to ensuring that the company gets value from the auditing efforts in the cybersecurity space. This will take some work, though.

The audit department has the potential to waste lots of your time, with little improvement in security to show for it. This can be frustrating. You know the areas in which auditors could provide value, but rarely do they ask for your opinion. If your audit team does ask for your opinion, consider yourself lucky. Make every effort to be a part of the audit-planning process, and as each audit kicks off, try to steer the auditors in the direction of the greatest gaps in cybersecurity. Your intention here is to partner with the audit department to help focus its efforts on those areas where you need help to move security forward.

A Typical Encounter with Auditors When Not Guided by InfoSec

To illustrate my point on how misguided the audit department can be when not partnered with the InfoSec team, here's an example from my past. I had been at the company for only a few months when "a helicopter virtually landed on my desk." No one gave me any notice it was coming. There was no email or meeting invite. The chopper descended, and a bunch of suits jumped out and informed me I was needed in a conference room. I found my way to the conference room, filled with people from corporate audit and one of the well-known auditing firms. Nice suits, combed hair, bleached teeth, and friendly smiles. These were auditors. Paid to ask questions. Paid to follow the checklist.

The meeting was formal and ceremonial, a kick-off meeting for our annual IT audit. I said nothing. The only one who spoke was the lead consultant from the external auditing firm. It wasn't until the very end of the meeting that I made the mistake of speaking up and offering to help. I suggested we work together to ensure the findings "made sense." I should have known better. My offer was dismissed without much consideration. I should have known that collaboration isn't a tool an auditor often uses.

The head auditor barely acknowledged my offer and assured me his team could handle it. I asked for a copy of the audit checklist (areas they would be auditing), but was told they'd focus on network security. I replied that was a broad area, and were there any specific areas they wanted to look into? I tried but got nothing other than the standard "We'll call you if we need any help." The meeting ended as pretentiously as it had begun. I shook hands with the attendees and returned to my office. The helicopter took off.

Remember, in Chapter 5 I said alignment to company culture is one of the keys to your success. I should have heeded my own advice in this situation and not been bothered by the auditors' unwillingness to partner. I was only trying to ensure they spent time on areas within network services that truly needed help. But collaboration isn't a remit of the audit department. This was one of those moments when I would need to just follow the process and submit to the audit department's direction. I'd taken the first step, but was shot down, so my inner voice told me to back off and see how this played out. Often alignment means stepping back, purging some of your ingrained beliefs, and adopting new ones that jibe with the culture and environment.

The audit lasted six weeks. During that time, I heard virtually nothing from our audit department or the auditors working the project. There were no check-in meetings, no findings to be clarified, no status emails, and no progress reports. Silence. Then finally, unannounced again, a meeting was called for that afternoon.

This time, more auditors were present. They arrived as if their work was of national importance, carrying secrets of grave consequence. Folders were held tightly to the chest and sealed. Few spoke or greeted one another. We filed into the same conference room where we'd met weeks before and took our seats. The guy at the head of the table that day was from audit headquarters. The attendees all looked in his direction as if looking at the great Oz shrouded with smoke and flames. I took my seat and waited.

One of the auditors distributed a heavy slide deck to the attendees. I weighed the report in my hands. It was thick, and I thought they must have uncovered some serious stuff. I flipped through it quickly, not wanting to disrupt the meeting. The presentation was formal.

As the meeting started, I prepared myself for bad news. The meeting moderator began. Audit finding number one: a switch was found to have the manufacturer's default password still in use. Audit finding number two: a closet containing network gear was found to be insufficiently secured. Audit finding number three: the network services team had little documentation of the network design....One insignificant finding after another. Each finding was read as if someone was being sentenced to prison. After the seventh finding, I began to wonder if they would have anything significant in their report.

The list of 15 or so items didn't amount to much and posed little risk to company security. I looked around the table at all the auditors. For six weeks, they had been living in local hotels, and this was the sum total of their findings? I was saddened at the waste of company resources. Not a single item on the list was worth talking about. All the findings were of low severity. Items overlooked by busy network engineers in the course of their daily routines. Sloppy housekeeping. Hygiene issues. Nothing I or the company should be concerned about. So here I was with the audit department as my teacher, and little improvement in security to be happy about. This is a clear example of one of my biggest problems with an audit: it often produces findings that are distracting and waste valuable resources.

I listened intently as the lead auditor continued to wrap up the meeting and his presentation. I could tell he'd given this pitch many times, but everyone sat politely and listened. No one seemed bothered by the insignificance of the findings. Maybe this was a good thing. Perhaps my colleagues had wised up to the value of an audit and realized it was safer to say nothing, and to simply march in place until the auditors left.

After the monologue was over, the lead auditor from headquarters asked if there were any questions. I couldn't believe my mouth was moving and out of it I was asking a question; I asked the head auditor if he'd had the chance to look at the architecture of our DMZs. The head auditor looked at one of his young staff members along the side of the room for the answer. A quiet yes was offered. There was some nervous commotion. I asked how many of the DMZs at our internet POPs they looked at? More nervous commotion. One had been audited.

Then I asked if they had reviewed the architecture of the one they'd audited. Again, the answer was a sheepish yes. They found the security architecture to be compliant with the company standards and industry best practices. Really? I asked if they noticed we didn't have any IDSs installed? "None?" they asked. More commotion. The lead auditor looked again at one of the youngsters on the sidelines. People around the table began to squirm a bit in their chairs.

An IDS, a key control spelled out by policy, is difficult to miss. These systems were fundamental to security. One of the most basic devices in the InfoSec architecture was nonexistent in our DMZs, and no one noticed. Yet they had pages of worthless findings, and pomp and circumstance like you've never seen. The meeting ended awkwardly.

I watched as the lead auditor carefully collected every copy of the findings he'd had earlier so ceremoniously and proudly distributed to all attendees. The room was silent and a bit tense, as the lead auditor indicated they'd be reissuing a new report within the next couple of weeks that contained a more thorough summary of their findings.

They had been professionally shamed, although this was not my intent. Even after this meeting, no auditor stopped by to see me or inquire about our IDS systems. The IDS issue did get added to the final report. And for my "collaboration" I did become the recipient of weeks of harassment from our audit department about the missing IDS systems. In the end, getting IDS systems installed was a win for the company, but being beaten by the audit department for a follow-up action item I provided was bittersweet.

Partnering with the Audit Team to Influence Change

To get value out of the audit process, you have to learn how to partner with the auditors to leverage their ability to influence change. If not properly aligned with the InfoSec process, an audit is often an impediment to the advancement of security, since most system owners can outwit auditors. You've probably seen this many times: an auditor asks questions of one of the IT engineers, and the engineer totally blows smoke the auditor's way while giving them no valuable information. Auditors are outmatched and don't have the experience in IT or cybersecurity to hold their own with an experienced engineer.

If I had kept my mouth shut during the meeting with the auditors, the report sent to our corporate office would have reflected only a few small housekeeping items. We would have cleaned up the discrepancies and been no more secure than we were before the audit began. Little improvement would have been made. But this would have been a colossal waste of everyone's time.

The challenge for the InfoSec team is to help the audit team in such a way that the company benefits from the time spent on audits. This isn't an easy task. It can take a long time to build a relationship of trust between the two groups, in which the auditors are willing to allow InfoSec to weigh in on their processes. One of my soft goals is to be a part of the annual audit-planning process. If I ever get to this point, I feel as though I've done my job and sufficiently partnered with the audit team. This isn't easy to achieve, however.

Where Did Auditors Get Such License?

Why is it that a corporation will fly a half dozen auditors across the country, put them up in expensive hotels, and pay exorbitant fees to receive a final report that contains few to zero findings of value? The short answer is fear.

After the Enron and WorldCom meltdowns, audit firms capitalized on the new laws and offered audits that "promised" to protect companies and the public from misrepresentations in the financial reporting system. Naturally, these new laws contained large sections devoted to IT and InfoSec/privacy, as they supported the integrity of the company's financial reporting system. To ensure that the public was not ripped off again by fraudulent financial reports (like Enron's), audit firms stepped in to provide a level of assurance that public companies were adhering to the audit firm's long checklist of security controls lifted right out of some industry framework or playbook.

Fearful companies bought up these compliance packages to avoid the possibility of fines they might receive for noncompliance. Few questioned the checklists or considered what the laws were trying to accomplish. Because of fear, companies bought into the "audit is important" mentality and have paid dearly for it. Inexperienced auditors became IT auditors and then branched into IT security, the latest hot market for auditors. Rather quickly, an army of auditors was formed.

A general Sarbanes-Oxley Act (SOX) audit consists of a set of questions that ask for things that often have nothing to do with the integrity of the company's financial reporting systems. Occasionally, I've tried to reason with auditors in the spirit of collaboration but have learned that no amount of reason will steer them from the safety of their audit checklist. They hold on to their checklist ferociously, never wavering from the topic of what they've come to audit.

The intent of the SOX law, enacted in 2002 in the shadow of the Enron and WorldCom debacles, was to ensure that a company's financial reports were processed over systems that were free of tampering and that protected the integrity of the financial reporting process. The results of the audit process of the financial systems would allow a shareholder to read the company's reports and rest assured that the numbers were accurate—a good and reasonable expectation.

This turned out to be a colossal waste of money spent by public companies. In a desire to comply with the law, companies hired IT financial auditors to ensure that their companies complied with the law's demands. Companies felt they needed a sheet of paper from an external audit firm attesting to the soundness of their process. This became a huge financial boom for audit firms.

The problem was that the law relied on the belief that lawmakers knew how to ensure a system's integrity through the written mandates of the law. They assumed that if we audited the systems, security controls were in place to ensure accurate financial reporting. Unfortunately, this is simply not true. In the first five years after SOX was enacted, no company had been fined for any violations, and yet in late 2008 we had the largest financial meltdown ever. I often told our chief financial officer we'd save more money paying the SOX fines than paying for the annual SOX audit.

Do you think I'm being too hard on auditors? Consider your own experience. Can you honestly say that after the auditors have left, all the reports have been issued, and management has chased their tails addressing the findings, your company's systems or data are any more secure? I cannot.

Audits have the potential to be disruptive to the valuable work being performed by the InfoSec team. The InfoSec staff knows the weak areas of security. Auditors do not. And auditors seldom ask the InfoSec team for input on the annual audit plan. This is where you should focus your efforts. Do your best to be a part of the annual audit plan. This will ensure that the audit department's efforts are focused on areas that move the security needle toward greater improvements in security.

Getting Value from an Audit

The secret to effective partnership with the audit team is to spend time on the relationship between the two departments. If you put some effort into this relationship, audits can be used to improve security—a goal you both share. To achieve this, cultivate a relationship with the audit department and aim to strike agreement about your mutual interests. You know where the security holes are in your armor, and if you can steer the auditors toward those holes, you really help the company. Both departments have the same desired outcome for the company. Playing on the same side makes the most sense.

I've had one relationship with an IT auditor that truly worked. He'd learned the value of always checking with me before he started any IT audit. When the time of the audit came, he would visit me and ask for my thoughts on the upcoming audit. He was looking for buried carcasses. We would review the audit checklist together. I would highlight those areas that I thought he should focus on. We in InfoSec knew where to look, and he was the one with authority to peek under the hood.

If I encountered teams that repeatedly refused to own the security in their area, the audit department was my tool of last choice. What a difference it made to have an auditor in my corner who could influence system owners for improved security. Sometimes it's best for system owners to hear from auditors after they've repeatedly ignored the InfoSec team. The audit department holds the ultimate hammer.

Auditors who blindly follow their generic lists will never know where to shine the flashlight. Auditors worth their salt know that partnering with InfoSec has the potential to yield the best results. If the auditors in my network services example had partnered with me, I would have discussed the areas of greatest need (in this case, the absence of IDSs), and they would have avoided embarrassing themselves in front of their boss. I still can't say an audit is worth all the time and money, but in partnership with InfoSec, you have an opportunity to use it for good.

Conclusion

Unfortunately, most audits begin with an air of distrust. The auditors come in with the assumption that something is amiss, and it's their job to uncover it. At the same time, IT often feels like the auditors are out to get them and report their shortcomings to management. Most auditors feel successful when they have something of substance to report. Getting the word that your department is getting audited is never a good feeling.

One of the goals of any good InfoSec department is to partner with the auditors to improve those areas of security that are truly lacking. Identifying those areas will not come from the audit department, but from the savvy InfoSec team that is able to partner with the audit team to use them for good. Unless the audit and InfoSec teams are aligned, the audit focus areas will do little to move the security needle forward. Unfortunately, the audit standard operating procedure does not include collaboration, so it will be up to the InfoSec team to build the relationships necessary to make a difference.

It's worth the effort, though, to develop good working relationships with the auditors. With patience, you'll learn you can use them to cause positive change in areas of IT where you may have been previously unable to do so. Do all you can to partner with the audit department for the sake of your company. It's well worth the effort. You just may find that this group can be a useful tool to open doors previously sealed shut to you and your team. The audit department has that ability. Partner with them wisely, and good luck!

12

A Note to CISOs

Many CISOs aren't successful in their jobs. Few last very long, and those that do usually simply survive rather than thrive. If you read the industry trade news, the average tenure of a CISO is just a little over two years. Year 1 is a grace period. Year 2 is a bilateral epiphany between the company and yourself that you're not the right person for the job. Year 3, the company is in discussions about how to replace you, while you're updating your resume and searching for a new position. Sound familiar? I see and hear about it all the time.

Time and again, I've seen CISOs pushed out of their jobs because of their approach to security or because they were overly insular and territorial about their work. I've been consistently amazed at the number of security professionals who are well intended in their approach but completely misguided or misaligned with their organizations. They're aliens to the company's culture, spending their time trying to move the company in a direction it doesn't want to go, all in the name of security. Despite all their good intentions, they view themselves as martyrs, believing they're fighting the right fight, while what they're actually doing is wasting their time and their employer's resources.

Is there a secret to thriving and not just surviving as a CISO or security leader? I believe so. Regardless of your tenure, you can apply the concepts of my seven-step process and improve your team's approach to InfoSec while strengthening customer relationships.

In this chapter, I'll speak directly to you about the fundamentals of your job beyond the seven steps, which are really focused on building and sustaining an InfoSec program. Some of what I propose might shake your foundations a bit, but I hope you're willing to challenge your models. Helping you and your team become a valued and respected asset to your organization depends entirely on your willingness to examine your current approach and possibly change the way you work to move your company toward a shared model of InfoSec.

Seeing the CISO as a Cultural Change Agent

As the CISO, your primary job is one of *cultural change* through education and adjusting people's attitudes about InfoSec. Your job is *not* to secure the company's information assets for the company, but to get the company employees to secure their information assets that support their business process.

You'll never be properly resourced to secure the company's information assets, and I'm recommending you not attempt to do so anyway. You don't own any business systems. Only the departments do. Only department management and their supporting IT staff can agree to partner with the InfoSec team to secure their systems. Without their consent, you're dead in the water.

To get in and partner with them, you have to approach them and have something to offer. So how do you influence each department to partner with you?

Your job is to influence and educate every department to take appropriate steps to secure their information assets. This can take some time, but it won't happen unless you get out of your office and knock on doors. This is a very different approach from the one that assumes that your job *is* to secure those assets.

Although you have to own the process of securing assets to get it done, the foundation of your job is to enlist others in the process. This applies to everyone in the company. The IT engineer, the gate guard, the HR rep, the scientist, the sales representative—every person needs to know their responsibilities toward protecting the digital assets of the company. If they don't know them, we can't expect they'll do their part. The big question for you becomes, "How do I enlist others?" How do you tweak their interest enough so they'll want to do their part?

An important concept to keep central to all your efforts is that your fundamental approach to effective InfoSec is based on relationships. This is the bedrock. Regardless of how your company views relationships, you have to be willing to make them foremost. In my experience, success won't come your way without really positive working relationships, so they have to be your focus.

If you're a CISO who wields a big stick, the clock is ticking on your tenure. Enjoy the ride 'cause it ain't gonna last. As the agent of change for your organization, you need to be the motivational speaker, the evangelist, and the catalyst for getting your company pointed in the right direction regarding real information security. You may not personally possess all the skills to be that kind of an upfront charismatic leader, but what you value, and where you invest your time, money, and staff, can make you a leader who can create a security culture in your organization. And if you choose to enter into this process, I can almost guarantee that you'll be around for a long time and will see the fruits of your efforts.

Most employees believe that somebody else is keeping their information safe, that security is somebody else's job. They believe the IT department is protecting our systems and our data. It's not, however. The IT department is providing some general security controls, but they have no idea where your data resides, or who has access to it, or how long you'd like to keep it around, or where it gets stored. This is beyond their job purview. Many staff members are just unaware of the threats to their information, the value of computer resources, and their own role to keep them safe.

As an agent of cultural change, you must shape the company's values and shift people's attitudes about InfoSec. You do this by helping people understand that the most important asset a company owns is the information resources used by its staff members. While this statement may seem broad and overarching, this task can be effectively accomplished through the steps discussed throughout the book: building relationships, broadening awareness and education, training staff, and never letting up on communicating the message of security. You'll notice there's not one technical pursuit in the foregoing list.

The CISO who operates as a cultural change agent takes a fully different approach to their work than those who are merely focused on the technical components of our trade. For the CISO focused on cultural change, each and every meeting becomes an opportunity to move staff in the direction of greater degrees of security awareness, and to educate those in the meetings on the threats associated with the information assets under their control.

One day, I was approached by a young woman who attended our two-day InfoSec conference. She said she saw the conference advertised in the company's weekly newsletter and had attended the whole event. She was excited about what she learned and was eager to get our help. I asked what she needed from my team and was taken aback by what she said.

She was in charge of a team of auditors who worked in the research department to ensure third-party research firms were living up to their contracts and protecting the results of research appropriately. The work her team (of about 10 people) was performing was basic InfoSec work, and they needed help. What she wanted was education for her staff, a CISSP-like course.

I couldn't believe her request. She stated she was uncomfortable with the data security practices of the other firms she audited, but she and her team didn't always have enough knowledge to identify poor InfoSec practices. She wanted customized training for the then 10 domains so her staff could do a better job and hold these other companies to their contract agreements.

We developed a training program for her. We gave the training to her staff in multiple sessions over several weeks. This was a huge win for the InfoSec team and a huge win for the company. All of this transpired because we held a security conference in the company's conference center and brought in industry-leading speakers and security professionals.

The point of my story is this: here was someone in the far reaches of the company who attended one of our security events, and the education she received would lead to the education of all her staff and improve the overall security for the company. These results are hard to refute. Everyone wins. This is the type of cultural influence that is part of your job description. We established a great partnership with her team going forward as they attended every training class we offered.

It's examples like this that reinforce the seven steps and my belief that the CISO's primary role is one of cultural change agent. If it was an isolated incident, I wouldn't hold this belief about our role, but the multiplicative effect security training can have far outweighs the value of any technology implementation. Whether we like it or not, we're cultural change agents.

Keeping Your Sword Sharp

Throughout my career, I've been blessed to work with talented engineers. I've loved working with these security hobbyists, whom we pay to perform their hobby at work. These types love to play with new technologies and are always learning. I've learned so much from them.

As a manager and leader, I'm always trying to improve my game. To do so, I read various trade magazines or management journals from leading educational institutes, as I need to stay on top of the technology and changes in management science. Both help me to think of creative ways to apply the leadership and management principles to the discipline of InfoSec.

Probably the smartest guy I've ever worked with is Ron Dilley, who worked with me as the security team's technical lead for over 10 years. I've learned more from Ron than anyone else in our industry. I'm grateful he took the time to explain all the technical stuff in simple terms I could understand. I was fortunate he worked with me as long as he did; he could've worked anywhere, and for more money than I was able to pay him. Try to surround yourself with people like Ron. They have a lot to teach you.

As the CISO, if you're not a technologist, you need to learn the basics of the profession. Whatever it takes, learn the technology. Read everything in the SANS reading room. Watch their webcasts. There is so much free education available on YouTube; dive in. You don't have to be a techie god, but you should be familiar with all the basic tools and processes your team is working with: firewalls/VPCs, network switching, the Open Systems Interconnection (OSI) stack, VoIP, wireless networking, encryption and key management, databases, operating systems/SD-WAN, programming languages, IDS/IPS, network scanners, hacking tools, virtual systems, malware, SDLC/Agile development/DevSecOps, code analysis tools, and more. My advice to you is to do whatever it takes to learn the tools of our trade. Your team will respect you for it.

Second, don't try to play a technologist if you're not. Stay in your lane. Know your place on your team. Your job as the CISO, as I've stated, is really evangelism and moving the culture to be more sensitive to InfoSec. My staff members know way more than I ever will. It's why I hired them. I always listen to them and their recommendations. Respect their recommendations. Your role is to ensure that their recommendations are well implemented and staffed, and that the proper groups are involved in the decisions your team is making.

Your last skill is to be a great communicator, facilitator, listener, and speaker. You *have to* carry the message before the team ever will. You *have to* be front and center. You have to set the example on collaboration, modeling what it means to be a good corporate citizen, evangelizing staff in the name of security, leading training sessions, and more. Staff members have to see you doing it before they'll follow and do it themselves. If you're asking them to man a table in the company cafeteria, you better be there with them handing out the brochures and talking to people. I'm a big fan of Level 5 leadership practices. If you don't know anything about them, bone up on the leadership model (*https://oreil.ly/oLp7K*) developed by Jim Collins in his book *Good to Great* (HarperBusiness) The team is more likely to follow you if you're coming from a place of kindness and humility.

For two years, I did all of the new-hire presentations every week. Each 10-minute session had anywhere from 15 to 30 people, and it was a good way to set the tone on day one for new hires. I made it a habit to take one of our team members with me to mentor them on public speaking. For public speaking to be effective, it must meet the three "F's." It must be funny, factual, and fast. I took our junior folks so they could see how I did it, including the jokes I used, how I answered questions, and the style I employed.

After a few presentations, all of them wanted to go it alone (an indication I'd hired correctly). I'd let them run the new-hire presentations for a couple weeks and then train another. It was a wonderful model, and our team learned how to give presentations through the new-hire sessions.

I still take courses on public speaking and push myself to speak at conferences and industry events. I often don't have the time, or necessarily want to address a particular audience, or speak on a certain subject, but I force myself to do it anyway. I've found over time that my best talks are humorous and to the point. This is my style: funny, fast, and factual. No one wants to listen to me. I keep this in mind. I don't have much to say, so I'd better say it quickly and leave them laughing if I ever hope they'll remember any of it. Public speaking will be one of the keys to your success. Refine the skill and don't ever stop working on it.

One of the CEOs at a company where I worked said the greatest business skill a leader can develop is public speaking. The CEO also said it was the one skill that enabled a person to get promoted faster. If you're able to stand in front of a group and communicate clearly and influence them, the sky is the limit for you, the CEO said. This message has stuck with me. I've done team-building exercises where we record our presentations and then watch them as a group. This is super humbling, and fun. Team members who can help each other and laugh at each other form close bonds. Evangelism is fundamental to your job description. Therefore, the art of public speaking can't be ignored.

Hiring Techies

Who to hire, who to fire? Putting together a team of real professionals is difficult work. Knowing the type of people to hire requires some consideration as to the journey ahead and the type of security program you want to build. If your department were just about the technology, hiring would be an easy task. You'd hire very technical people, deploy rock-solid systems, and provide insightful analysis for the company—end of story.

But the task in front of you is not that narrowly defined. You and your team must reach out to every group in the company and provide services that vary from team to team. The job description for most IT or engineering teams is straightforward. It usually involves providing the same service to different customer groups. For example, the team responsible for supporting mail/messaging services has one platform to support, and it's the same platform for everyone in the company. The desktop team provides the same or a limited number of desktop clients to the company. These groups provide the same or a few platforms to everyone. Window administrators provide the same build over and over, followed by system administration.

Regardless of the IT group you look at, you will find a tightly defined job description. This is simply not the case for the security team. To the legal department, your team is the investigative arm they use to retrieve data from any system in the company. You're also the source of knowledge for policies the company desperately needs. To the operations center, you are the leaders of every security incident, providing analysis for all incidents. To the network services team, you co-own the many network security tools in the environment. To corporate security, you are the forensic team. To the desktop team, you provide consulting on the latest endpoint security suites and encryption tools. You provide continual pentest services to all departments, and the results are often of interest to the legal and audit departments. The financial control team looks to you for SOX compliance, and the Health Insurance Portability and Accountability Act (HIPAA) squad wants general computer controls (GCCs) to protect health-care information.

To all system owners, you provide many services, from patch management to encryption. The list goes on and on, and as I discussed in Chapter 1, probably no one outside your team appreciates the variety of services and the depth of knowledge required to be successful.

No other IT group has to adjust its approach and be subject-matter experts to such a diverse set of audiences. In light of this, do you really want to hire individuals who are merely technologists? Do you really want a heavy-headed employee who lacks interpersonal skills? I don't.

When hiring, I follow a few simple principles that protect me from making a bad decision, and I've rarely made a mistake in hiring. Following my process, you can get through resumes quickly and conduct phone screens in five minutes.

Rule number one: new hires *must* have a technical degree (for example, computer science, electrical engineering, math, or physics) from a school you can drive to. If you hire people with solid degrees, they will easily grasp the concepts needed to go anywhere in the IT security space. They'll have the underlying theory of how computer systems work.

Note

I'm leery of the Management Information Systems (MIS) degrees, or any of those flavors, because these degrees end up being a curriculum of all introductory courses. They lack depth in any one discipline and contain little theory about what's happening on the wire, disk, or software.

I also like to hire engineers who have worked for companies with name-brand recognition. I've found that those who work at bigger companies know the rules of the road required to navigate big company environments. Change management is a huge consideration in every project that people from small companies don't get exposed to. Likewise, decisions made at headquarters need to be thought through for various countries, laws, and cultures. Engineers from small companies don't have this level of experience.

If they have those two boxes checked—a technical degree and big-company work experience—I schedule a 10-minute phone screen for my drive home. I use this phone call to ascertain whether a candidate has solid communication skills. From the initial greeting, I can usually tell whether they're confident, outgoing, and positive. I ask them a few nontechnical things, and then we delve into some technical areas. From this short call, I can tell if I'd like to meet them in person.

One of my best hires was someone I may work for one day. They're that kind of a natural leader—engaging with a great wit. They're comfortable in any setting and have a gift for making people laugh. The real kicker is they're also very technical; they love the geek stuff! I've often said that if I had three folks just like them, I could go anywhere and be hugely successful. They like to snowboard and take a lot of sick days in the winter; funny how they always get sick after a storm dumps four feet of powder in the Sierras. They're so talented, though, they can have all the sick days they want. They happens to also love their job and the work I ask them to do for the company.

I make sure my team members know the hiring process well. I recommend you develop the hiring criteria as a team. It can be fun team-building exercise, and the discussion among the team helps reinforce why we hire the talent we do. It becomes a source of pride on the team when they realize we have some of the most capable people in the company. I remind them of this often. If you hire with those two traits in mind, you increase your chances of putting together a team that is capable of living by the values I've laid out in this book.

Note

Even with this simple set of hiring principles, I typically screen about 40 people before I find a promising candidate. There are lots of posers in our field. Hiring is that important, 40:1. It takes time to find talent, so don't ever stop looking—even when you don't have any openings.

Hiring people who can "go anywhere" is critical to your success. There's not a person on our team who I wouldn't let go talk to the CEO by themselves. Even our new college hires are confident, personable, and technical enough to be left on their own. They all know the importance of listening first, not speaking down to anyone, and gently influencing to achieve a goal.

I can rest knowing my team will be out all over the company, and will be great ambassadors for our InfoSec team and our program. I'm confident of it. It wasn't long ago that the most junior member of the InfoSec team taught a class to 50+ staff members on "Wireless Security at Home." Unbeknownst to us, the CIO was in attendance. When the class ended, they sent me an email about how much they enjoyed the class and how good the teacher was. The CIO had no idea this guy was only a year out of college. They asked to meet the young man one-on-one. This was proof that our hiring process works! How many 23-year-olds get the chance to provide training to the CIO of a Fortune 100? Not many.

Utilising Lunches

Anyone who has ever worked with me knows that I love the power of team lunches with other groups. Every InfoSec budget I've ever submitted has a line item for lunches. Three per week is 150 lunches per year, at $150 each, for a budget of $22,500. This will honestly be your best money spent.

There is no more powerful tool than breaking bread together. Do it as often as you can and use the time to connect with others on a personal level. Find out about their lives outside of work, their interests, where they used to work, places they've lived. Listen and ask lots of questions. People love to talk about themselves, so let them.

A good rule of thumb is that every new connection you make with another group in the company should be done over lunch. People throughout the company are a little leery to meet with the security team. Disarm them over food. After introductions around the table, ask everyone to share their favorite movie or Netflix series and you'll begin to build the bonds of friendship. I remember more from these lunches than any conversation I have with people in the hallways. It's also a great way to get a long list of must-watch Netflix shows. So do lunch with your colleagues.

FREE LUNCH FRIDAYS

Here's a practice that will come back to you in spades, and it's easy to do. Vendors are knocking at your door to demo their products, so take them up on their offers but require that they host a lunch for whatever number of people you want.

The vendors don't care. They need to get in front of potential clients, so hosting a lunch at your company scores them big points on their side.

Show some wisdom in the companies you invite for lunch. If you're trying to push the company in the direction of a certain technology, bring in the top players in that space to host lunches with those who would use the systems. This is just lunch, and you know how techies love to eat.

I always get on the phone with the vendor before the day of the lunch (Friday) and game the presentation a bit. We discuss the points they should hit and who will be in attendance. I also dictate the menu. Otherwise, everyone would bring pizza or sub sandwiches. No, I request PF Chang's, Chipotle, Thai food, and other specialty foods beyond fast foods. The vendors love it, and meanwhile you're influencing the dialogue with regards to a direction you believe another team should consider.

An example of a successful round of vendor lunches was with the data sciences team where I worked. I met with the team frequently, and each time we met, I got different answers regarding the management of the company's sensitive data. As a security guy, these conversations are unnerving. I suggested we crawl some of the data stores, looking for sensitive data types, but couldn't get any traction. It was frustrating.

The next move was to host a series of vendor lunches from the leading vendors in the data governance and data discovery space. I lined up three lunches over the course of a couple of months (never do them back-to-back). After the second vendor lunch, the data sciences team was signing up for a one-month proof of concept to test out the vendor's tool. Voila! After the third vendor lunch, we were doing a bake-off among products and heading down the procurement path. This was InfoSec judo at its finest.

My rule of thumb for vendor lunches is this: I try to do 3 per month, or 36 for the year. Most happen on Fridays. I've used them to educate my team, influence other teams, and help steer discussions we've been having with other groups about directions we'd like to see them go. They're easy to pull off, so go for it.

Pick the vendors that make sense, meaning those whose tools you're interested in, or those whose tools would be good to learn about, and use the time for education in a specific area. These are free events that cost you only the transaction time to schedule the meeting with the vendor. As I said earlier, I always had pre-meetings with the vendors to set expectations, which ensured our time wasn't wasted. I would also always invite people from across the company, and some lunches have upward of 20 people. The more, the better!

LUNCHES WITH OTHER COMPANIES

Hopefully, you work in a geographical area that has a concentration of other large companies. (Most of my career, I was in Washington DC, Los Angeles, or Silicon Valley.) If so, they too have InfoSec teams you can connect with and learn from. When I worked in Silicon Valley, I was in heaven. The world's leading tech companies were one or two exits away. I aimed to take my team to meet with eight other companies a year.

To set up these lunches, reach out to the CISO and propose a team meeting in which you bring some members of your team to their office with lunch in hand. Sit down with this other team for 90 minutes and benchmark all you're doing against what they are doing. You'll be amazed at how rewarding this time is.

While I worked in Silicon Valley, we met with many of the big-name companies. This was a huge win for my team as we got an inside look at other InfoSec teams from the likes of Facebook, Google, eBay, Netflix, Twitch, Splunk, Evernote, Box, Dropbox, Salesforce, Zynga, and many more. We were able to make great friendships with these teams. The benefit to you and your team is that you get to ask them lots of questions. Everyone we met with really helped us. We also learned a lot from top-notch engineers.

Through these meetings, I also met some wonderful mentors. I often would go back and have lunch with just the CISO to learn more from them. My all-time favorite meetings were with Rich Tener from Evernote. Rich taught me to how to use our bug bounty program for all our pentest needs. The guy is brilliant, so having lunch with him a couple of times a year was a no-brainer for me. I also think of Demetrios Lazarikos, "Laz," the founder of Blue Lava, and previously the CISO at Sears. He's been a mentor for years. To think I'm on a first-name basis with these individuals is humbling.

I also think of Joel Dela Garza, formerly at Box, now with Andreessen Horowitz, another mentor whom I followed up with after our team meetings. The list goes on of other CISOs who taught me a lot: Jason Chan from Netflix, Chris Deibler from Twitch and now Shopify, and Aanchal Gupta from Facebook and now Microsoft. All three spoke at our cybersecurity conferences, and I never would have met them if not for our team lunches. Make company team lunches a habit, and I promise that you and your team will be blessed for doing so.

Holding Cybersecurity Conferences

Remember that I said in Chapter 7 that education was your road to success? If you believe this, I suggest you host a cybersecurity conference at your company. They're free and fairly easy to plan and execute. Your company's staff will really enjoy them as well.

I did my first conference back at Amgen in 2004; a Microsoft sales guy told me that Microsoft liked it so much, it started hosting its own conference every year, called BlueHat. I would get the best speakers possible: SANS instructors, local CISOs, FBI agents, and CISOs from a few of our key vendors. I would offer multiple tracks and breakout sessions. These conferences didn't cost us any money, as I would ask one or two key vendors to pick up the tab, and preclude them from bringing any more than two guys. While at Amgen, we had about 15,000 staff members working at our Los Angeles campus, and about 1,000 of them attended at least one session from our conference.

These conferences can be a huge win for the company and your team. And the only investment you need to make is the time required to plan the event.

Meeting with Other CISOs

Here's another no-brainer: get together with the CISOs in your local area. If you can get three or four of them, invite them for drinks at a local restaurant or hotel bar and just talk shop. I would prepare a list of topics to discuss and then meet them at a five-star hotel for drinks and hors d'oeuvres.

My all-time favorites are Jonathan Chow from NBC Universal and now Live Nation; Bentley Au from Toyota North America and now AEG; Craig Froelich, formerly at Countrywide, now at Bank of America; and Anne Kuhns from Disney. I look up to all these individuals, as they've taught me so much, and the price to me was a little LA traffic and a $150 bar tab. I met with them frequently throughout my 15-year stay in LA while working at Amgen, Warner Bros., and KPMG.

Meet with other local CISOs and pick their brains. Everyone likes to share what they're doing. You can instantly benchmark your program against theirs, and you get an inside look at how to do things in a different, and often better, way. Also, if you hold these meetings regularly and spend a few hours together, you don't need to go to any conferences, as this compressed amount of time investment will keep your skills sharp.

Conclusion

I don't consider myself to be very smart, so I needed to come up with creative ways to differentiate myself. These tricks made a huge difference in my career and in the InfoSec programs where I've worked. I hope you find them useful. I have many more tricks up my sleeve, but to get them, you'll have to contact me directly. Good luck on your professional journey.

Final Thoughts

I hope I wasn't too much of a blowhard throughout the course of this book. I do get passionate about InfoSec and feel strongly about the seven steps I've laid out. However, not all of the steps are of equal importance. So if you have time to do only a few of them, focus on the following steps, for which anything less than excellent execution spells trouble for you and your program.

First, step 1, cultivating relationships, will determine the quality of the program you build, as you will be allowed to build only the program your relationships permit you to build. Let this point sink in. Relationships will, by and large, determine your tenure and your success at work. Those who don't think highly of you are most likely actively undermining you. Your job is hard enough when everyone supports you, so having detractors will make the job grueling. If you have poor relationships with anyone, I recommend pulling out all the stops to mend those as soon as possible.

The next focus area should be step 2, ensuring alignment. If you're not properly aligned with the company's culture for risk, or the company's ability to support your function, then you're probably building a program the company doesn't want or need. Being this misaligned will lead to heartache and pain for you and your team. Do your best to realign quickly, following the few simple suggestions I provided in Chapter 5.

Third is the importance and value of having a communications program, step 4. This area cannot be overemphasized. Strong communication allows you to reach areas of the company where you wouldn't normally go, and to reach staff in ways you wouldn't otherwise be able to. In the original writing of this book, the communications chapter was twice the size of the next longest chapter. That's how much I value communications and know of the multiplicative effect it can have on your efforts and program.

Finally, one of the best things you can do to help your program succeed is to spend time thinking about this last domain, or the art of our trade. No doubt you spend most of your time in the eight domains already, so incorporating some of these softer pursuits can only add to the job you're currently performing. I think you'll find that the items I've highlighted will enhance your efforts within the eight domains and will be a win-win for you and those you're partnered with.

Where to Go from Here

The beauty of my seven step-process is its simplicity. It touches all the essentials of your position and keeps the truly important elements, like relationships, at the forefront. Whether you're just starting a new position or evaluating an existing InfoSec program, you can use these seven steps to ensure you're focused on the right areas.

The questions going forward are: Where do you go from here? How do you apply the seven steps to your existing or new program? The seven steps are a road map for getting you up and running, a guide to keep you focused on what truly matters as you implement and grow your program over time. Using the seven steps, you can get a quick evaluation of the health of your program.

If you have a well-established InfoSec program, these seven steps can be used as a quick assessment of your fundamental processes. For those with mature organizations, here are some basic questions to ask yourself and your team:

Step 1, cultivate relationships:

- Do I have good working relationships across the organization?
- Are there relationships that need to be improved?
- If so, how?

Step 2, ensure alignment:

- Is the InfoSec program aligned with the risk tolerance of the company?
- Is the program supporting the various risk profiles of the individual business units?
- Am I, as a leader, aligned with the risk tolerance of the company and leadership?

- Does my request for resources align with what the company is willing to pay for InfoSec?

Step 3, use the four cornerstones:

- Do we have the proper foundational building blocks for an InfoSec program? What about documentation (policy, charter, SIRP)?
- Do we have the proper security architecture in place, and is there a road map going forward?
- Do I have adequate governance processes in place to stay aligned with the business and to keep the business side of the house involved in InfoSec decision making?

Step 4, create a plan for communications, education, and awareness:

- Do we have a communications plan for the year?
- Do we have a communications, education, and awareness program?
- Are all departments targeted with specific messages clearly spelled out?
- Does the communications plan include phishing?
- Do we offer technical training courses to the product and engineering teams?
- Do we have general communications targeting staff members?
- Are all the InfoSec team members involved in the communications plan?

Step 5, give your job away:

- Is the InfoSec team actively partnering with others throughout the company to secure the company's information assets?
- Have you given InfoSec responsibilities to other teams?
- Is the InfoSec team regularly meeting with other teams to discuss industry frameworks?
- Are there any RACI charts for shared InfoSec responsibilities?
- When you review industry frameworks, do you acknowledge that InfoSec functions and responsibilities are "owned" by other engineering teams?

Step 6, build your team:

- Are all the team members good communicators?
- Do they have outstanding technical competencies?
- Are they assigned to various business units and technical teams?

Step 7, measure what matters:

- Are you capturing the metrics that matter to address the board and company leadership about the ROI made in InfoSec?
- Are you tracking the staff's ability to respond to phishing emails?
- Can staff throughout the company recognize policy violations when they happen and know how to report them?

Asking just a few questions will give you a pretty good feel for the health of your program. Be honest with yourself, or better yet, take your team through these questions. If you score poorly in the relationships area, you should either update your resume or put together a plan for how to turn those relationships around.

If you follow my process, all the technical topics will surface during your "lunch tour" when you present the NIST, OWASP, CIS Top 20, or other industry framework to the IT and engineering teams. Then the road maps for each area will naturally fall into place and the path forward for both your team and the IT/engineering team will be codified.

Conclusion

An InfoSec department that values and pursues relationships gains trust from other departments by the value and respect the InfoSec team members extend to their colleagues. Contention won't foster the atmosphere needed to work together and will be counterproductive to getting work done. Don't allow any of your team members to be contentious. Defer to and advise the clients on security leading practices. Allow your business partners to make security decisions. The victory is that your client groups are implementing their *own* security controls. Hopefully, tomorrow they'll take it even further. Strive for incremental progress while supporting the business.

My advice to you is don't be the feared colleague whom people succumb to because they are afraid of what you might do. Be the person others trust and value, a trusted advisor willing to shine the light on others to make them look good as they move security forward.

If you've learned nothing else in this book, I hope you've at least come to understand that successful InfoSec requires just as much art as science. Perhaps you've noticed that nowhere in this entire book have I given advice about the technology needed to make your information assets more secure. That's because you cannot secure the company's information assets by simply buying better and more technology. All of the steps I've laid out in this book will do more for increasing the security of your information assets than any technology ever could.

This process has been effective for me because it applies a management art to an area requiring engineering science. It provides a well-defined process to help navigate the ill-defined job of leading an InfoSec function. The most difficult piece of this process is getting your team to quit seeking solutions in technology and to pivot to securing company assets through relationships, education, and awareness training.

I've learned these seven steps on the job. I still use them to this day—because they work. If you're willing, you can do it too. It may require that you honestly examine your approach, let go of some old and possibly bad habits, listen to the feedback your team gets from the organization, and require that your team be open to change.

Finally, treat everyone with kindness. Kindness and humility working together go a long way. Overlook the invisible middle fingers. Go where you're wanted. Work with those willing to work with you. View your work in terms of laps around a track. Remember, the InfoSec job is an uphill marathon. Bring in professional training courses to enhance the skill sets of others. Practice evangelism often.

If you practice just some of these, you'll be acknowledged and valued for the positive contributions you make to the company. Others will notice. Good luck!

Index

About the Author

Todd Barnum is the chief information security officer (CISO) for GoPro Inc. Todd started with GoPro in 2015 and is responsible for the company's cybersecurity efforts, which secure and protect information important to GoPro and personal to its customers. Todd came to GoPro following CISO positions at Warner Bros Entertainment and AMGEN Inc. He also led cybersecurity consulting practices for KPMG LLP and Forrester Research.

Earlier in his career, Todd served as a naval officer and held a variety of technology and cybersecurity leadership positions. While living in Los Angeles, As an Adjunct Professor at California Lutheran University, Todd taught computer science courses in the undergraduate and graduate programs. Todd also served as a Board member of the Ventura County YMCA, and volunteered with Orange County's Big Brother Big Sister Program.

Todd holds a master's of science degree in information technology from the Naval Postgraduate School and his Bachelor's from the University of Hawaii. Todd is the father of one son.

Colophon

The cover illustration is by Susan Thompson. The cover fonts are Guardian Sans Condensed Medium and Gilroy Bold and Semibold. The text font is Adobe Minion Pro; the heading font is Adobe Myriad Condensed; and the code font is Dalton Maag's Ubuntu Mono.

www.ingramcontent.com/pod-product-compliance
Ingram Content Group UK Ltd.
Pitfield, Milton Keynes, MK11 3LW, UK
UKHW031555170425
457563UK00008B/76